Self-Discipline

Blueprint to Success in 10 Days for Entrepreneurs, Weight loss and Overcome Procrastination, Laziness, Addiction - Achieve Any Goal with Powerful Long-Term Daily Habits and Exercises

Stephen Patterson

© Copyright 2019 - All rights reserved.

The content contained within this book may not be reproduced, duplicated or transmitted without direct written permission from the author or the publisher.

Under no circumstances will any blame or legal responsibility be held against the publisher, or author, for any damages, reparation, or monetary loss due to the information contained within this book. Either directly or indirectly.

Legal Notice:
This book is copyright protected. This book is only for personal use. You cannot amend, distribute, sell, use, quote or paraphrase any part, or the content within this book, without the consent of the author or publisher.

Disclaimer Notice:

Please note the information contained within this document is for educational and entertainment purposes only. All effort has been executed to present accurate, up to date, and reliable, complete information. No warranties of any kind are declared or implied. Readers acknowledge that the author is not engaging in the rendering of legal, financial, medical or professional advice. The content within this book has been derived from various sources. Please consult a licensed professional before attempting any techniques outlined in this book.

By reading this document, the reader agrees that under no circumstances is the author responsible for any losses, direct or indirect, which are incurred as a result of the use of information contained within this document, including, but not limited to, — errors, omissions, or inaccuracies.

Contents

Introduction _____ 1

Chapter 1:
The Power of Willpower _____ 3

Chapter 2:
Human Behavior and Self-Discipline _____ 13

Chapter 3:
Motivation _____ 39

Chapter 4:
Facing Failure _____ 51

Chapter 5:
Developing Good Habit Fundamentals _____ 61

Chapter 6:
Vocabulary for Success _____ 73

Chapter 7:
Strategies for Self-Discipline _____ 87

Chapter 8:
Controlling Your Environment _____ 91

Chapter 9:
Develop Drive _____ 95

Chapter 10:
Directing Your Attention _____ 99

Chapter 11:
Social Motivation _____ 105

Chapter 12:
Measuring Progress _____ 111

Chapter 13:
Don't Weigh Pros and Cons _____ 117

Chapter 14:
Keeping Your End in Mind _____ 121

Conclusion _____ 123

SELF
DISCIPLINE

Blueprint to Success in 10 Days for Entrepreneurs, Weight loss and Overcome Procrastination, Laziness, Addiction - Achieve Any Goal with Powerful Long Term Daily Habits and Exercises

Stephen Patterson

Introduction

Willpower is a person's ability to control their desires, attention, and emotions. People have started to realize that willpower plays a vital role in their success in every aspect of their life. Everybody understands that they are supposed to have control over every area of their life, but a lot of people feel that they are failing at that.

The American Psychological Association believes that a lack of willpower is the main reason why people struggle to reach their goals. A lot of people feel guilty if they let others or themselves down. Others are at the mercy of their own cravings, thoughts, and emotions. They live their lives based on impulses and not conscious decisions. Even people that have their life together end up feeling exhausted at holding everything together, and they start to wonder if things are really supposed to be so hard.

Willpower and self-discipline are what helps people feel in control of their life without feeling stressed about it. This isn't something you can develop overnight. It will likely take you quite a while before you completely understand what it means to be disciplined. But it can be done, and you can do it.

In this book, you will find information about building daily self-discipline that can be used in all areas of your life. This book is about turning you into a person that is disciplined every day, and you will be able to successfully use this for growth. Besides learning how to become more self-disciplined, we will also look at different ways to become stronger mentally. It can sometimes feel hard to have to push through those obstacles, especially if you don't think you have enough willpower, but this book will provide you the tools you need to knock over those obstacles and keep going.

Chapter 1:
The Power of Willpower

Everybody mostly thinks that their life can be improved if they had a bit more of the mysterious thing known as willpower. With a little bit more self-control everybody could stop procrastinating, save for retirement, avoid drugs, stop drinking, exercise more, and eat right. The American Psychological Association performs an annual Stress in America Survey. They ask their participants, among several other things, about their ability to make reasonable changes in life. Their number one reason for not following through with changes is lack of willpower.

While most people blame a lack of willpower for their problems, they have not entirely given up hope. Most people who responded to the survey felt that they could learn willpower. They could be right. Research has recently found ways that willpower can be strengthened. But there were survey participants that felt that more time for themselves would improve their willpower. That is probably not going to help them out anyway. Scientists, over the past few years, have made some discoveries about how willpower works.

Willpower is not the only reason why a person may not reach their goals. Roy Baumeister, Ph.D. and psychologist described three critical components for achieving a person's objectives. First, you need motivation for the change and a clear goal. Second, your behavior needs to be monitored toward the goal. The third is willpower. No matter if your goal is to spend less time on social media, study more, kick a bad habit or lose weight, willpower is an integral part of achieving your goal.

Willpower basically can resist short-term temptations so that you can reach long-term goals. There are many different names that we give willpower: self-control, self-discipline, resolve, drive, and determination. In psychological terms, willpower tends to be defined as:

- A limited ability that could be depleted.

- Conscious regulation of the self that takes effort.

- Being able to use a "cool" cognitive behavior system instead of a "hot" emotional system.

- The ability to be able to override unwanted impulses, thoughts or feelings.

- Having the ability to delay gratification and resist temptations to reach long-term goals.

One hundred thousand years ago, for people to survive, they had to find food, avoid predators, and reproduce. Being a part of a tribe increased their odds of survival. Taking somebody else's girlfriend or dinner could jeopardize their lives, but also the life of the tribe. Self-control was essential for survival back then and played an important part in evolution.

Willpower is already present in all of us since we were born, but not many can use it effectively. An efficient and straightforward test was conducted by a psychologist, Walter Michel, to determine the willpower amongst children. It is called the marshmallow test.

A plate of marshmallow was presented by Michel's team to the preschoolers. The children were informed that they would be left alone for a few minutes and if they were able to wait until the researcher came back in, the child would get two marshmallows. If the children decided to ring a bell to bring immediately back the researcher because they couldn't wait any longer, they would only be given one marshmallow.

Thirty years after the initial test, the team followed up with the children. They have observed that the children that waited for the second marshmallow have been living a better life and have high scores on SATs and lower BMI. Self-control has proven to be a good indicator of academic achievement over intelligence, a better determinant of good leadership over charisma, and is more critical for marital satisfaction over empathy. People that have more willpower tend to be:

- Healthier
- Happier
- Have better relationships
- Make more money and better off in their careers
- Can manage stress better and deal with conflict

Neuroanatomy

The prefrontal cortex is located just behind the forehead and eyes, and it controls our behavior, thoughts, and abstract thinking. This means that it helps in mediating conflicting ideas, enables you to make choices between right and wrong, and predict the outcome. Naturally, it controls the things that we pay attention to, thinks about, and feel.

The prefrontal cortex has grown significantly during human evolution, which tells us that there was an intense selection pressure that helped it to grow and evolve. Let's put this into perspective. The last five million years has increased the brain about three-fold. At the same time, about six-fold has been grown by the prefrontal cortex.

The prefrontal cortex is the last part of the brain to mature. The development of this part is likely to be finished when it reached approximately 25 years old.

This is probably the reason why sensible and intelligent teens take part in excessive or high-risk behaviors even though they know the possible outcome.

To help you understand the importance of the prefrontal cortex for willpower, let's look at what can happen when it's damaged. Phineas Gage's story is a prime example. In 1848, at 25 years old, Phineas Gage was working on the rails as a foreman. He was a well-respected man and considered to be respectful and quiet. His physician said that he was active both physically and mentally.

Unfortunately, something went wrong when he was working a routine procedure on September 13. A tamping iron with the length of seven inches has pierced through Phineas' skull and somehow damaged his prefrontal cortex. Surprisingly, though, he didn't die and made a full recovery in a few months. However, something was not right and very different, although his wounds have healed. His friends and colleagues have observed the change in his personality. Dr. Harlow, his physician, said this about his change:

"The balance between his intellectual faculties and his animal propensities seems to have been destroyed. He is fitful, irreverent, indulging at times (...) impatient of restraint or advice when it conflicts with his desires..." It is said that he lost his willpower when he lost his prefrontal cortex. There are still more things that can damage the prefrontal cortex aside from accidents such as this. Being distracted, sleep-deprived or drunk can leave us less equipped to help with our impulses. If the prefrontal cortex controls how we question whether we need an expensive pair of shoes, then what controls our impulses and cravings? It is said that on our minds, two people are living. This is based on some neuroscientists.

There is the good one who takes the long-term goals into their account, and the other one is the spoiled one who wants instant gratification. Everybody has both, and we switch between the two from time to time. The primitive brain is what neuroscientists call the area of the brain that is in control of our desires and cravings. The hippocampus, hypothalamus, and amygdala can be found on the primitive brain. This area controls your long-term memory, motivation, behavior, and emotions.

When a willpower challenge happens, like with the marshmallow example, the primitive mind will scream for that candy, but then the prefrontal cortex jumps in and reminds us that we would prefer two pieces of candy.

Willpower is in a constant clash between these two systems. Walter Michel, the researcher behind the marshmallow study, created a framework they referred to as the "hot-and-cool" system that explains how willpower will either fail or succeed. Your cognitive and thinking system is called the cooling system while your impulsive and emotional part is the host system. The hot system controls the responses to specific triggers.

Strengthening Your Self-Control

There has been much research conducted over the recent years that have looked to explain all the different facets of willpower. Most researchers who explore self-control have the same goal in mind: How can we make willpower stronger? If willpower really is a limited resource, as other research has suggested, what can you do to conserve it?

Staying away from temptation is one great way to maintain self-control. In the marshmallow study performed by Walter Michel, the children who sat and stared at their treat was a lot less likely to resist that treat than the children who shut their eyes, looked away or found a way to distract themselves. This "out of sight, out of mind" idea also works for adults. One study was able to discover that office workers who had candy in the desk were less likely to indulge than if they placed their candy on their counter where they could see it.

Another good way to help improve self-control is what psychologists refer to as "implementation intention." Typically, these intentions will take the form of "if-then" statements that will allow people to be able to plan for moments that could end up foiling their resolve. For example, if a person is watching their alcohol intake, they may tell their self before going to a party, "If somebody offers me an alcoholic beverage, then I will ask for club soda with lemon." Research that looked at adults and adolescents found that implementation intentions can improve self-control, even for people who have had their willpower depleted by lab tasks. Coming up with a plan of time could end up allowing you to decide within the moment without having to use your willpower.

The research that suggests that we might possess a limited amount of willpower causes a few troubling questions to come up. If we are faced with a lot of temptations, are we going to fail? Not necessarily. Researchers don't think that a person's willpower can ever be entirely used up. Instead, people appear to keep hold of a reserve of willpower that they can use for future demands. With the right motivation, we can tap into those willpower reserves, which will allow us to persevere even if out self-control has been run down.

Mark Morven demonstrated this idea and found that willpower-depleted people were able to persist on self-control tasks when they knew that they would benefit other people or be paid for the efforts they exerted. This means that high motivation could help a person overcome weak willpower, at least to a certain extent.

Willpower may be less vulnerable to depletion. Researchers who have studied self-control have described willpower as a muscle that can become fatigue when used a lot. But there is another part to the muscle analogy. While muscles do become exhausted, they will strengthen when regularly used over the long term. This means that periodically exerting self-control could end up improving the strength of your willpower.

Morven and his colleagues, in one of their first demonstrations, asked participants to follow a two-week regimen of tracking their food consumption to help their posture and mood. When compared to the control group, the people who exerted more self-control by doing their assigned exercises were not as likely to experience willpower depletion in the follow-up tests.

In another one of his studies, he discovered that smokers who used willpower for two weeks by staying away from sweets or regularly using handgrips ending up being more successful. The successful participants gave up smoking while control subjects who went on two weeks performing regular tasks that didn't require self-control on their part, like writing in a journal did not.

Other people have also been able to prove that flexing your self-control muscle can strengthen the willpower with time. Australian scientists Ken Cheng Ph.D. and Megan Oaten Ph.D. of Macquarie University in Sydney gave participants a two-month exercise program, which was a routine that would require them to use willpower. At the end of the program, the participants who were able to stick to their plan ended up doing better on the lab follow up of self-control than the other participants that didn't get assigned an exercise regimen. That's not the only thing either. The participants also said that they smoked less and drank less alcohol, ate healthier foods, monitored their money spending, and improved their study habits. Working their self-control while working out led them to have better self-control in almost every area of their life.

With the discoveries that suggest willpower depletion is connected to the glucose levels, they tell us that there may be another remedy. Eating regularly so that the blood-sugar levels in the brain are maintained could help to refuel willpower. Dieters who aim to keep their willpower without reducing calories may do better when you eat frequent small meals instead of skipping lunch or breakfast.

All the evidence from the willpower-depletion studies has also shown us that creating a long list of resolutions on New Year's Eve is probably the worst thing you can do. Being depleted in an area can lower your willpower in other areas, so it only makes sense that you should concentrate on just one goal in a single time. That means, don't try to start an exercise program, adopt a healthy diet, and quit smoking all at one go. It's best to take your goals in a one by one approach. After you have gotten a good habit in place, you will no longer have to draw on your willpower to keep performing this behavior. Eventually, following healthy habits will be your normal routine, and you won't have to decide at all.

Chapter 2:
Human Behavior and Self-Discipline

Self-control is what separates us from our ancestors and the rest of the animal kingdom. As you know, this comes from the prefrontal cortex of the brain. There is of debate within the science field as to whether willpower is a finite resource. This is what is known as ego depletion.

Some studies have found that exercising willpower requires a lot of mental energy, especially on the reserves of glucose, which is the fuel the brain prefers. This all can lead to depletion or weakened willpower. The central concept of this ego depletion is one reason why people are more apt to grab a cookie when they feel stressed out and not when they feel on top of the world.

Recently, though, scientists have been unsuccessful in replicating some of the studies that underlie ego depletion. There is more research underway, but the verdict on if you can "run out" of willpower remains to be seen.

If you remember the marshmallow study from the last chapter, the results seemed to indicate that willpower is an innate ability, but reviews, later, suggest that our willpower changes over our lives and it can be improved with practice. Having a better understanding of why we tend to cave to some impulses, but we can resist others, is crucial for obtaining an understanding of eating disorders, impulsivity, and addictive behaviors.

Whether you find that you are most tempted by scrolling through Facebook, sex, food or drugs, we all have different areas in life where we could use a little bit more willpower. There are ways to strengthen your willpower, which is what you will learn throughout this book. Some of the most common ways to increase willpower are through mindfulness, routines, and rewards. Strengthening willpower isn't always easy, but the benefits can improve your quality of life, work performance, and health. We're going to look at how willpower affects different bad habits and how you can work through these habits.

Procrastination

Procrastination is something that we all face at some time in our life. For as long as humans have existed, we've had to struggle with avoiding, delaying, and procrastinating on things that matter. While we are productive when we have figured out how to not procrastinate, we feel accomplished and satisfied.

Alright, let's figure out what procrastination is. Procrastination is such a timeless problem. The term Akrasia was even created by Socrates and Aristotle to describe this behavior. When you act against your better judgment, you can call it Akrasia. Even though you know that you should be doing something different and may be important, you still do something else.

It's great to have a definition, but why do people procrastinate? Behavioral psychology has found what is known as "time inconsistency," which explains why we all fall prey to procrastination even though we have good intentions. The tendency of the brain to value immediate results more than future rewards is what is known as time inconsistency.

Think about it this way. You have two selves: The Present Self and Future Self. When you create goals, such as learning a language, losing weight or writing a book, these are your Future Self's goals. You are trying to prepare yourself on want you want in your life in the future. When you think about the Future Self, as scientists have discovered, the brain will notice the value in taking actions easier with long-term benefits. These long-term rewards are what the Future Self likes.

However, the only one that can act is the Present Self, no matter how the Future Self loves these goals. Your Future Self is no longer there when you decide. Since you are now situated in the present time, the Present Self is now what the brain is concentrating on. Scientists have found that the Present Self does not like much the long-term rewards compared to instant gratifications.

This puts the Future and Present Self at odds a lot. While the Future Self likes to be trim and fit, the Present Self says otherwise and wants to eat a donut. Everybody knows that they need to eat healthy now so that they don't wind up overweight ten years down the road, but risks like heart failure and diabetes are still far away.

Similarly, no matter how well most young people know it is essential to save money for their retirement when they are still young, they again can't act because they feel that the payoff is still decades away. Instead of saving the money they used to buy expensive shoes for the future, the Present Self even purchases the shoes anyway.

Therefore, you still go back to old patterns in the morning, even though you feel motivated to change your habits before you go to bed the night before. When the rewards are set to happen in the future, the brain prefers these long-term benefits. However, when the mind is in the future, it prefers immediate gratification. Keeping your Present Self-motivated cannot rely on consequences and long-term rewards. It's important, instead, to figure out how to move the rewards and punishments to the present. The future results must be made as present consequences.

An important note about the action line is that as soon as you are over that line, your pain will start to go away. In fact, staying in the middle of procrastination tends to be more painful than being in the middle of the work. The anxiety, guilt, and shame that you experience while you are procrastinating tend to be worse than the energy and effort that you must put into the actual work. The problem lies in starting the job, not doing it.

There are many ways that you can stop procrastinating.

Make Your Reward for Action Immediately.
If you can make it seem that the benefits of your long-term decisions are immediate, procrastination can be much easily avoided. One great way to do this is to use a strategy known as temptation bundling.

Katy Milkman came up with temptation bundling through behavioral economics. This strategy suggests that you bundle an excellent behavior in the long-term along with good practice in the short-term. Some good ways to bundle temptation are:

- When you have monthly meetings, you can prefer to only hold it on one favorite restaurant.

- Only enjoy your favorite show while you do chores or iron.

- While processing work emails, you can get a pedicure.

- You can exercise and listen to audiobooks at the same time.

The Consequences Should Be Made Immediately

There are several ways to make you forcefully face the consequences of your procrastination right now instead of later. For example, you can exercise with your friend so you will be compelled to work out and not be a jerk if you miss one out. This is much better than just working out alone where you may tend to be lazy and not exercise at all.

Create Your Future Actions

A favorite of psychologists is to use a "commitment device." These will create, ahead of time, a future action. One example would be to buy food that is individually packed instead of buying things in bulk to help curb your eating habits. You can also remove your applications and games on your cell phone so you will not waste time. These are just some of the many ways on how commitment devices can help reduce procrastination.

Create Achievable Tasks

The thing with procrastination is that it is hard to start the behavior or even change the current one. Reducing the size of the habits is a good idea because it will be easier to start when they are smaller. By these, it will make you procrastinate less.

A great way to make a habit easier is with the two-minute rule. This rule says that "When you start a new habit, it should take less than two minutes to do."

The goal is to make it much easier for you so you can quickly get things started and trust that you can finish the task through the momentum. It will be a lot easier to continue a job when you start performing it. That's why the 2-minute rule helps you to overcome laziness and procrastination by making tasks much more accessible to begin so you don't have the time to say no.

Along the same lines, you can break your tasks into smaller sections. Take, for example, Anthony Trollope. He has published two plays, 12 short stories, 18 works of non-fiction, 47 novels, and several letters and articles. How was he able to achieve this? Instead of looking at his progress through finished books or chapters, he looked at his development in a fifteen-minute time span. His goal is that within 15 minutes, he should write 250 words. He continued this every day for three hours. This way, he felt satisfied and accomplished every fifteen minutes, while he was working towards the goal of finishing a book. So, we've looked at beating procrastination daily. Now, we need to make this productivity a habit that will last for a long time and prevent procrastination from returning.

We slip back into procrastination because no system will determine what needs to be finished first and what is essential. The best productivity system we are going to look at is called The Ivy Lee Method:

- At the end of the day, write out six things that you need to get done tomorrow. Only six, no more than that.

- Prioritize the six things in order of real importance.

- The next day, focus on the first thing on your list. Work until you have finished that first task before you start the second one.

- The remaining items on your list should be worked in the same way. When you have unfinished items on the list after the day ended, those items should be moved back to the top list for the following day.

- This should be repeated daily.

This is a great way to get started beating that procrastination habit. You can only make willpower work for you if actual start working.

Addiction

Addiction can be classified as a person engaging in behavior or the use of a substance where the reward provides them with a compelling incentive to repeat the action despite the possible negative consequences. Addiction can involve things like nicotine, cocaine, opioids, inhalants, alcohol, or behaviors like video games or gambling. Scientific evidence shows that addictive behaviors and substances share key neurobiological features; they activate intense brain pathways of reinforcement reward, many of which involve dopamine.

Addictive behaviors tend to be accompanied by mental health conditions like anxiety and depression or other pre-existing issues. These addictive behaviors not only use a lot of the same brain mechanisms of compulsivity, but they also respond to similar treatments.

There isn't a single cause of addiction, although biological factors like genetics could contribute to the vulnerability to the problem. Many environmental, social, and psychological factors influence substance use as well. There isn't a single personality type that can be associated with addiction. The only thing that can link to addiction is the ability to tolerate strong feelings like distress.

While all addictions tend to cause a sense of hopelessness and feelings of failure, as well as guilt and shame, research has found that recovery is the rule and not the exception and that there are several different routes to recovery. This road to recovery isn't going to be straight: relapse or recurrence of use is very common, but it does not mean it's the end of the road. For people who can achieve remission for five years has the likelihood of relapse that isn't any greater than the general population. To diagnose an addiction, their need to be at least two of the following things present in the person:

- The activity or substance is used in large quantities or for a period longer than was intended.
- There is a want to reduce use or unsuccessful efforts to do so.
- The pursuit of the activity or substance or recovery from it takes up a lot of time.

- They have a strong desire or craving to perform the activity or use the substance.

- The activity or substance use disrupts obligations at home, work or school.

- Their activity or substance use continues despite their interpersonal or social problems that it creates.

- Participation in important recreational, social or work activities stops or drops.

- Use tends to happen in situations where it is risky.

- Use will continue despite knowing its cause or exacerbates psychological or physical problems.

- Tolerance occurs. This is known either through a need to diminish the effect of the same amount or increase the amounts to achieve the desired result.

- Withdrawal happens and manifests either in the presence of withdrawal symptoms or the need to take something to block them.

The severity of the problem is gauged by how many symptoms are present. Two to three symptoms mean there is a mild problem. Four to five symptoms mean there is a moderate problem. Six or more symptoms indicate that the condition is severe. There are many different biological, environmental, and psychological factors that can contribute to a risk of addiction.

Scientists believe that genetic factors can contribute to about half of the risk of developing an addiction. There is a factor that links to vulnerability due to a variation in a gene that determines the brain's receptor makeup for dopamine. Another factor could be the nature of the hormonal response to stress.

Physiological factors can play a part in addiction. A variant in liver enzymes that metabolizes different substances could influence alcohol abuse.

Gender is also another big factor. Males tend to be more likely to develop substance abuse disorders, although this "gender gap" could be narrower for alcohol abuse, and females tend to be more prone to intoxication effects at a lower amount of alcohol.

A person that tends to be a sensation seeker and impulsive is at a higher risk of addiction. Impulsivity is mainly related to a risk of relapse.

A person who has suffered through trauma or abuse is also at higher risk. Perhaps, through sensitizing the brain pathways of distress and alarm due to the added burden of stress, early exposure to large amounts of adverse experience can contribute to developing a substance abuse disorder because the coping ability has been overwhelmed.

Mental health problems like PTSD, ADD, anxiety, and depression increase the risk of addiction.

A strong family relationship has been shown to reduce the risk of substance disorders, but many different aspects of family circumstances or functioning can contribute to a higher risk of addiction. If you have a sibling or parent with an addictive disorder, the risk higher, as does a lack of parental support or supervision. Troubled parent-child relationships and family disruptions increase risk. Research has found that marriage and child-raising responsibilities mitigate addiction risk.

If a person has easy access to alcohol or other substances in their home, at work or school, it increases a person's risk of repeated use. The people you hang out with also increases your risk of use. If you're around people who use, especially during the teenage years, you are more likely to develop an addiction.

Lastly, employment status plays a part. Having a job and growing your skill set exerts pressure for stability and provides you with psychological and financial rewards that help to mitigate the chance of addiction. While there are many different types of addictions out there, we're going to look at the three common addictions and how to overcome them. We won't go back through the symptoms because addiction symptoms are the same no matter the addiction.

Video Games

Overcoming a video game addiction, much like all other addiction, can be difficult. However, with enough time, a person can learn to enjoy playing video games without being addicted. The following tips could help a person overcome their addiction.

Do not quit cold turkey – Video games, unlike other addictions, take up a lot of time. Quitting altogether can leave a large space in a person's life, and can cause a person to relapse, sinking them further into their addiction. The goal should be to curtail the amount of time that is spent playing the games.

Moderation – Come up with a specific number of minutes or hours to play video games each day. Set a timer and when it goes off, stop playing.

Lower the number of systems in the house – Between handhelds and consoles and other gaming systems, you can't play all of them in a limited time. A lot of people try, though. Instead, reduce yourself to a single system that you play games on. This will let you focus on one system without feeling like you must play a game on each one of your systems.

Stay away from MMO's – MMO's are the worst games to play if you have a severe addiction. They waste a lot of time. Some people have even died while playing them since they tend to play for days at a time without taking a break.

Schedule breaks – For every hour you play, stop, stand up, and take a walk for a few minutes. It's not good to sit in front of your TV for long periods of time without a break.

Limit the amount of money you spend on games – Allow yourself $60 or less each month for video games. This means you should only be buying one or two games a month. Limiting your spending will limit your addiction.

Pick games that require physical activity – There are more and more games that are becoming movement based. There are some that require you to stand and move around. They may still be video games, but they do encourage exercise.

Make it a family thing – There are plenty of games out there that families can do together. This will let you play games while also spending time with family. Remember, though, that you should teach your children moderation. This could end up increasing an addiction, so it may not be the best option for you.

Get help – There could be some underlying issues as to why you're addicted to video games. Finding a mental health professional is a good idea and you should not be ashamed of it. A PCP could help you as well.

Figure out if you have other issues – Your video game addiction could be caused by some other problem in your life. Talking to a professional could help you find the other problem areas.

Pick up other hobbies – Create a collection, do gardening, and so on, just find something else that will keep your mind and hands busy. You can also include family and friends in some of these.

Review your life – Take a look at what your life is like right now. What areas could be better? Maybe you missed out on a job because of your addiction. You might have missed out on your child's school event. Try to right those wrongs.

If you still don't believe that video game addiction is real and is a big problem, let's look at the story of Shawn Woolley. In 2001, Shawn Woolley killed himself. His mother found him and found that the online game Ever quest was running. The mother blamed the game for his suicide, but the Sony CEO disagreed.

There isn't any proof to whether Ever quest resulted in his suicide. His mother believed that his addiction to the game and his death could have been caused by a possible love interest in the game. Unfortunately, there isn't any real proof.

Addiction may have been a big part in Shawn's death. Shaw also suffered from physical and mental health issues, which were likely worsened by the fact that he was always in front of his computer. He had stopped working, stopped interacting with family, and stopped paying bills.

It's hard to say who is to blame. His mother tried to help, and it's not Sony's place to make sure that people get help. But this should be proof enough that video game addiction is a real problem.

Shawn's mother, in 2002, founded On-Line Gamers Anonymous to help other people who are addicted to video games. It's up to the family and friends to confront the addicted person about their problem. Everybody must help the addicted person to take responsibility. You can't just say, "It's only a video game."

Alcohol
First, think about these statements

- It's how I unwind and relax after a long day.

- I have fun drinking.

- It's how I forget my problems.

- I would have energy and time for activities and people that I care about.

- I would feel physically and mentally better.

- My relationships will likely improve.

- It affects my job performance and responsibilities to my family.
- I often feel ashamed, depressed, and anxious.
- It has created problems in my relationships.

Once you have decided to change, the next thing would be to come up to establish clear goals. The goals need to be clear, specific, and realistic. You do not want your goal to be simple, I will stop drinking alcohol. Instead, your drinking goals should look something like this:

- I will not drink on weekdays, beginning on (insert date).
- I am going to limit what I drink on the weekends to no more than three a day and five the entire weekend.
- After three months, I will reduce my weekend drinking to a max of two per day and three the entire weekend.
- It helps to answer these questions:

Are you interested in quitting altogether or cutting back? If you only want to cut back, you should decide which days you are going to drink and how much you will drink? What day do you want to quit drinking or start drinking less? Once you have set your goals, write down a few ideas on how you are going to accomplish those things like:

- Remove temptations from your office and home.

- Announce your plans. It's important for everybody you are close with to know what you are doing. You can even ask others who drink to not drink in front of you.

- Be truthful about your limit. Let people know if you are no longer allowing drinking to happen in your house and that you might not go to events that will have alcohol.

- Stay away from bad influences.

- Learn from your past.

Whether or not you are going to be able to cut back on your drinking successfully will depend on how severe your problem is. If you are an alcoholic, meaning that you have no control over your drinking, it is best if you quit drinking entirely.

Some people can stop drinking on their own or with a 12-step program or support group. Others will require medical supervision to withdraw comfortably and safely. Which way you choose will depend on how much you drink, how long you have been struggling, how stable your living situation is, and any other health problems you might have. There are four main alcoholic treatment programs:

- Residential treatment means that you will live at a facility while you undergo treatment during the day. These treatment programs typically last 30 to 90 days.

- Partial hospitalization is for those who will require ongoing medical monitoring but have a good living situation. These programs will typically meet at the hospital for three to five days each week and normally last four to six hours.

- Intensive outpatient programs work on relapse prevention and are often schedule around a person's school and work.

- Therapy can be used to help figure out the root cause of your alcohol abuse, fix your relationship, and learn about coping skills.

No magic treatment will work for everyone. Everybody is going to have different needs, so it is crucial you figure out the program that works best for you. With alcohol abuse, you will have to face withdrawal from alcohol. This is something that doesn't necessarily happen with video game addiction. When you have been drinking frequently and regularly for a long time, your body will become physically dependent on the alcohol and will go through withdrawal when you stop. The symptoms can include:

- Elevated blood pressure and heart rate

- Trouble concentrating or sleeping

- Stomach cramps and diarrhea

-

- Restlessness and anxiety

- Vomiting or nausea
- Sweating
- Shaking
- Headache

These symptoms will typically start within hours of your last drink and peak in one to two days, and usually improve after five. For some alcoholics, withdrawal can be life-threatening. If you have been a long-term heavy drinker, you might have to be medically supervised during your detox.

Drugs

Recovering from a drug addiction works a lot like an alcohol addiction. Your recovery from any addiction doesn't start by stopping your use. Instead, it is done by creating a new life where it's easier for you not to use. Everything in your life doesn't have to change, but there are some behaviors and things that have been causing you trouble. These things, if you don't let them go, will continue to get you into trouble. The more you try to retain your old life during recovery, the less well you will do.

You can use the same steps from the alcohol section to overcome drug addiction, but here are a few other things you can do.

Try to avoid high-risk situations. One easy way to figure out if you are in a high-risk condition is to remember the word, HALT: hungry, angry, lonely, and tired.

How are you feeling at the end of the day? You will probably be hungry if you haven't eaten well. You might be angry if you have had a tough day. You could feel lonely if you're isolated. You don't have to be alone to feel lonely. And you are tired. This is going to be when your strongest cravings occur. Other ways to know if you are in a high-risk situation are:

- If you are around people that you use to use with
- People whom you have conflicts with or people who encourage you to use.
- If you are in a place where you used to use.
- If you have things around you that remind you of using.

You can't altogether avoid these situations, but if you are aware of them, you won't be caught off guard. This will help you to prevent your cravings from turning into significant urges. Taking better care of yourself will help. Make sure you have a healthy lunch, so you're not as hungry later. Join a 12-step program that you won't feel as isolated. Learn the best way to relax so that you can release your resentments and anger. Develop better sleeping habits.

People will withdraw from drugs just like they do from alcohol. The symptoms are all pretty much the same. Depending on your drug of choice and how long you have been using will affect your withdrawal symptoms.

Oversleeping

People often struggle to get enough sleep, so the issue of sleeping too much seems like a luxury. It's not. Just like insufficient sleep, oversleeping is a sign of disordered sleep. This problem could be connected to mental health. It could also mean that they have poor sleep quality, and a clinical sleep disorder could cause it.

Sleeping too much is also linked to many of the same health problems that are sleeping too little is related to, which includes cognitive issues, metabolic issues, and heart disease. People who sleep too much also have higher mortality risks. Hypersomnia is the clinical term for oversleeping, and excessive day sleepiness. Hypersomnia has a few core symptoms:

- Trouble concentrating
- Grogginess on and off through the day
- Trouble getting out of bed and beginning your day
- Difficulty getting up in the morning.
- Sleeping for longer periods of time at night.

Let's be clear that I am not talking about the once in a blue moon night of extra sleep. This can happen to everyone occasionally. If you keep your sleep routine consistent, it shouldn't happen that often. You're probably wondering how much too much sleep is. The tricky thing is that there isn't a single right amount of sleep for everybody. Rest is an individual need. The following are a few factors:

- Your genetics can influence your internal sleep drive and circadian rhythms.

- In your 20s, you may find that seven hours is enough, and you may need eight hours in your 50s or 60s.

- Sleep provides your body and mind with energy, so if you have exerted a lot of energy during the day, you will need more sleep.

- If you are working through health issues, you will probably need more rest. This is true for short-term and long-term conditions.

- Given your life circumstances, like periods of change or upheaval and stress, can temporarily increase your sleep need.

That said, most people during their adulthood will need somewhere between seven and nine hours of sleep. Some people may be good at six to six and a half hours, but it is improbable that you can function well at five hours of sleep or less. Similarly, some people need nine hours of sleep, but if you regularly sleep more than nine hours and you still wake up fatigued and tired, you could be oversleeping.

Teenagers and young adults will often oversleep as a sign of depression. It is difficult to gauge a teen's sleeping pattern because their sleeping habits are typically very different from adults. An estimated 40% or more people under 30 that suffer from depression will experience hypersomnia.

But, sleeping and depression have a complicated relationship. Disrupted sleep is a symptom of depression and a cause of depression. Most people that suffer from depression experience sleep disturbances. Sleep problems are also able to make depression more difficult and severe.

Sleep disorders aren't always seen as having a harder time sleeping. They can also interfere with the quality of sleep and can trigger oversleeping and excessive sleepiness. Any sleep disorder that causes sleep deprivation can cause excessive daytime sleepiness. Hypersomnia is closely linked to some specific sleep disorders:

- Narcolepsy is a neurologically based sleep disorder where the brain doesn't have any control over the sleep-wake cycle. People with narcolepsy tend to have excessive daytime sleepiness and strong urges to sleep. They will often have nighttime insomnia.

- Restless leg syndrome causes a creepy-crawly feeling in the legs. These feelings will often cause people to need to move their legs. RLS is normally more intense at night and often causes people to experience insomnia.

These people will normally experience daytime sleepiness and could oversleep because they aren't getting enough quality rest.

- Obstructive sleep apnea compromises a person's breathing during sleep. While sleeping, the airway becomes completely or partially blocked for a short period of time. This will happen several times and can cause frequent awakenings.

- Idiopathic hypersomnia means that a person is excessively sleeping for no reason.

Substance abuse can also cause a person to oversleep, as well as other medical conditions like obesity, Alzheimer's disease, epilepsy, brain injuries, MS, and Parkinson's disease. If you think you have hypersomnia, you should talk to your doctor. It's also a good idea to limit your alcohol intake and do your best to avoid becoming sleep deprived.

No Motivation

You don't feel that much interested in doing extraordinary things when you have low motivation. No motivation happens when you aren't interested in doing anything. You start avoiding friends, decline or cancel social events, stop hitting the gym altogether, go to work only when you must, and you may self-sabotage.

Now, there are times when no motivation as usual. This happens when you go through a significant life change like bereavement, breakup, or redundancy.

This is just when your mind needs a bit of a timeout. When no or low motivation has gone too far or may start endangering your life, it may become a mental health concern. Things to watch out for are:

- If it has gone on for over six weeks.
- If you don't know the reason why you don't be motivated.
- If you are experiencing suicidal thoughts.
- Is unchanged or worsened.
- If it is constantly accompanied by negative thoughts.
- If you start to lose interest in family and friends.

Considered as a big issue on mental health, depression can cause low motivation. Schizophrenia, acute stress reaction and bipolar disorder can also cause low motivation. If you are experiencing low motivation and you have an obvious trigger such as career issues or a life change, it is helpful to have self-help. If you cannot manage your low motivation anymore or it has already lasted long enough, it is now the time to talk to a coach or counselor.

Chapter 3: Motivation

Motivation is a mighty, yet tricky beast. Sometimes you may find that you get easily motivated, and you are wrapped up in a whirlwind of excitement. Then there are times when it is nearly impossible to figure out how you can get motivated and you feel trapped in a spiral of procrastination. This chapter will look at the best ways to get and stay motivated.

Don't worry, though, this isn't going to be some rah-rah pep speech. Instead, we are going to look at the science behind motivation and how you can keep yourself motivated. This could be figuring out how to motivate yourself or how you can motivate your team. Motivation is defined as a willingness to do something. It's a psychological force that compels you to perform some action. This is all science, but we can figure out a better definition of motivation.

Steven Press field, the author of The War of Art, described motivation as "At some point, the pain of not doing it becomes greater than the pain of doing it.". There will be a point where it is easier to change than to remain the same. It will be easier for you to act and feel insecure while you are working out at the gym than sitting still and experience self-loathing at home. It will become more comfortable for you to feel awkward while making sales calls than handling disappointed about your bank account.

This is the most basic definition of motivation. Every choice you make has a price, but when a person is motivated, it becomes easier to handle the inconvenience of the action than the pain you feel when you stay the same. Here's the vital question: what can we do so that we can make it more likely that we will pass that mental threshold and feel motivated consistently?

A surprising thing about motivation is that it tends to come after you begin a new behavior and not before. There's a common misconception that motivation comes because of passively consuming an inspirational book or a motivational video. However, active inspiration tends to be more powerful.

Motivation is typically a result of the action and not the cause of it. Getting things started, even if it's something small, is one form of active inspiration that will naturally provide you with momentum.

One great way of referring to this effect is the Physics of Productivity because it is merely Newton's First Law applied to habits: objects that are in motion will stay in motion. After you have started a task, it will be easier to move forward.

Motivation isn't needed as much when you start a behavior. Almost all the friction with a task will start at the beginning. Once you have begun, your progress will happen naturally. Thus, a critical part of getting motivated is making things easy to start.

A lot of people will struggle to find the motivation to achieve their goal because they waste too much energy and time on other areas of their process. If you are looking to make it easy to find your motivation and get things started, then you need to automate the early parts of your behavior.

Something a lot of people tend to do to delay work is to start to think about when they are going to do it again. This can be seen with habits like creating art, starting a business, working out, and most other habits.

- If you don't have a set time for when your workout is supposed to happen, then you will wake up thinking, "I hope I have the motivation to exercise today."

- If you don't have a marketing system for your business, then you will show up with your fingers crossed that you will figure out how to get the word out, as well as everything else you must do.

- If you haven't picked a time to write something each week, then you will often find yourself saying something like, "I just need to a bit more willpower to get stuff done."

Creating a schedule seems relatively simple, but it will put your decision-making in autopilot by providing your goals a place and time to live. It will be more likely that you will follow through no matter how much motivation you have. Also, there is a lot of research that has been done on motivation and willpower to back this up.

Quit waiting for your inspiration or motivation to hit you and create a schedule for the habits you want. This is what separates the amateurs and the professionals. Professionals will design a program and stick to it. Rookies will wait around until they feel motivated or inspired.

How are some of the most prolific artists in the world motivated? They don't just create a schedule; they form a ritual. Twyla Tharp is one of the greatest choreographers and dancers of the modern era. In her book, The Creative Habit, Tharp talks about role rituals and how they have affected her success.

For example, in her book, she explains how she wakes up each morning at 5:30 AM, gets dressed for the gym, walks outside and hails a taxi, tells them to take her to Pumping Iron gym, and then she works out for two hours. Her ritual in this is not the weight training or stretching that she performs. Instead, her routine is hailing the cab and telling them where to go. This act stays the same for every day and habituative it and makes it less likely for her to skip her gym time.

Mason Currey, in his book Daily Rituals: How Artists Work, talks about how a lot of the world's great artists follow a regular schedule.

- Maya Angelou would rent a local hotel room and would go there to write. She would get there at 6:30 AM and would write until 2 PM. She would go home and edit it. She never stayed the night.

- Michael Chabon, a Pulitzer Prize winner, writes from 10 PM to 3 AM five nights a week.

- Haruki Murakami gets up at 4 AM, spends four hours writing, and then goes for a run.

The most creative people don't depend on inspiration or motivation. Instead, they follow a consistent routine and pattern. The following are some examples of how you could create a method and ritual to help with your motivation:

- Sleep better – Keep a "power down" routine that you perform before bed.

- Start every morning stress-free – Come up with a five-minute morning meditation.

- Be more creative – Keep a creative ritual that you do before you begin singing, writing, painting, or whatever it is you do.

- Exercise consistently – Do the exact same warm-up routine every day in the gym.

The power of your pre-game routine is that it will give you a mindless way to start your behavior. It will make starting your different habits a lot easier, and this means that following through consistently will be more comfortable.

The key to creating a good ritual is that it will get rid of the need to come up with a decision. What will I need to do first? When do I need to do it? How do I need to do it? A lot of people won't get started because they aren't able to decide how they can get started. You need your starting behavior to be automatic and secure so that you will have the strength to finish it when it ends up being challenging and difficult. To make motivation a habit, three simple steps can take to do just that:

- A good routine will begin by being so easy that you aren't able to say no. There should be no need to be motivated to start your ritual. For example, to get started writing, I will grab a glass of water. You could start your workout routine by putting on your running shoes. These are super easy tasks and there is no way you could say no. The most important part of all tasks is getting them started. If you aren't motivated at the start, then you are going to find that motivation will start after you have begun. This is the reason why a routine must be super easy to start.

- Your routine needs to get you headed towards your end goal. Having a lack of mental motivation is often connected with a lack of physical movement. Picture your physical state when you are unmotivated, depressed, or bored. You don't move all that much. You could be slumped on the couch.

This opposite is true as well. If you make sure that you are physically engaged and moving, then you will feel energized and engaged. For example, when you are dancing, it's hard not to feel energized, vibrant, and awake.

While you want your routine to be easy to start, it's important that you gradually transition into more physical movement. Your motivation and mind will follow that movement. It's also important to understand that physical activity doesn't always mean exercise. For example, if you want to get writing, your routine should bring you closer to writing.

You must stick to the same pattern every time. The main purpose of your ritual is to create several events that you will always do before you start a certain task. Your ritual lets your mind know, "This is what happens before I do (insert task)." Eventually, your ritual will become so close to your performance that by performing that ritual, your mental state will be primed. You don't have to know how to figure out your motivation, you only must start your ritual.

If you have ever heard of the 3 R's of habit formation: reminder, routine, reward, your ritual is nothing more than a reminder. Your ritual is meant to trigger your habit, even if you don't have any motivation for it. This is extremely important because when you don't have any motivation, it will often be too much work to figure out what you need to do. When you must face another decision, you will typically choose to quit. However, having a ritual will solve this problem because you will know what you are supposed to do. You won't have to debate or decide. Lack of motivation won't matter. You follow your pattern. Here comes the critical part, learning how to stay motivated for the long run. We're going to do this with the Goldilocks rule.

Let's pretend that you're playing tennis. If you were to try to play a serious game against a child, you would soon find yourself bored. The match will be way too easy. But, if you were to try to play a game against a professional player like Serena Williams, Rafael Nadal, or Roger Federer, you will find that you are not motivated because it's too difficult.

Now, compare these two games with a game that you play against a person who is equal to you. As the game continues, you will make a few points and lose a few. You have a pretty good chance of winning, but only if you try. Your focus will narrow, and your distractions will disappear, and you will be invested entirely in the game. Your challenge will be "just manageable." Victory is possible but not guaranteed. Science has found that these tasks are more likely to keep you motivated.

Humans like to be challenged, but only if it is within their best zone of difficulty. Tasks that are under your abilities are boring, and functions that are beyond your abilities are discouraging. Tasks that are between the two are motivating. We want to be able to master a skill that is just beyond our current knowledge.

This is known as the Goldilocks rule. You want things that are just right. Working on tasks that fall under the Goldilocks rule is a key to maintaining your long-term motivation. If you discover that you feel unmotivated on a job, it is probably because it has floated into boredom or has become too complicated. You will have to figure out a way to pull that task back into your abilities where you feel challenged, but capable.

This exceptional blend of peak performance and happiness is often referred to as flow. Flow is what performers and athletes find when they find themselves "in the zone." This is a mental state where you are so focused on your task that everything else disappears. By following the Goldilocks rule, you will find yourself falling into the flow more often. But you will also need to measure your immediate progress. That means that measurement is an essential factor in motivation.

Hedonic Motivation

Hedonic motivation is the influences that come from a person's pain and pleasure receptors on their willingness to reach a goal or retreat from a threat. This is what is linked to traditional motivational principles where people will avoid pain and learn toward pleasure. This is gained through acting on certain things that result from emotional and esthetic feelings like joy, love, fear, hate, and so on. According to hedonic principles, emotional experiences can be viewed as a gauge that can range from good to severe and the primary motivation is to try to keep the needle as close to the right side as possible.

For example, writing a report for work could have two types of motivators. One would be that you write a great story and get a raise, which is the pleasure. The second would be that you don't and get fired, which is the pain.

Historically, avoidance and approach have been linked to hedonic beliefs of pain and pleasure. Hedonic comes from a Greek word that means "sweet," which means "relating to or characterized by pleasure." This makes it interesting because while the hedonic motivation incorporates pursuing pleasure and avoiding pain, the concept is often linked to the positive connotation of pleasure. One example would be hedonic goods are often bought so that the person can find enjoyment and satisfaction in the item, and this experience is often seen as hedonic experiences. Pleasure and pain are the body's natural compass. They point us towards what needs to be done and will help us to figure out if what we are doing will help us survive.

As hedonic motivation became popular, so did other types of interpretations and views. Socrates was one of the first to start studying hedonic motivation. He felt that it was a person who should follow a specific course of action where pleasure would exceed pain, and if they didn't follow the said path, it would be because they don't understand what pain or pleasure could result.

Democritus viewed hedonic motivation a lot as Socrates did, but he never had a definition of what things were painful and what was pleasurable besides that people avoided pain and liked pleasure. He felt that each person knew what they wanted and what they didn't like.

Epicurus thought that with hedonic motivation, pleasure and pain would even out, and people would learn how they should do things in moderation. Later, philosophers also created their interpretations of hedonic motivation.

Thomas Hobbes' explained hedonic motivation as people will generally work to avoid painful or adverse environmental events and approach those that are pleasurable or positive, this is also known as incentive motivation. Our learned remembrance on if something is unpleasant or pleasurable sets how we will approach an event.

Stephen Patterson

Chapter 4:
Facing Failure

For those who haven't heard, "There's no such word as can't," I wonder how things would work if we all believed that statement, especially when it comes to going after our dreams. Think about all the excuses people make throughout the day and how they keep us from going anywhere:

- What will people think?
- I don't know if I'm ready.
- It's too personal to share.
- I'm not as good as (insert person).
- I can't write.

In fact, we are all already capable and competent. All you must do is accept it. Do you remember the story about the little engine that could? Once he switched up his mindset, he was able to change his destiny. You have the power to do the same.

Remember what Henry Ford said, "Whether you think you can, or you think you can't – you're right." You must begin believing that you are able to do anything, no matter what it is. Let's try a little exercise.

Step 1
Create a list of all the things that you have been avoiding because you believe that you "can't" do it. This could be submitting an article to a popular journal or becoming a part of your local writers' group. It could be that you finally sign up for that class you have been avoiding.

Step 2
Now, spend some time imagining yourself doing those things. Picture yourself sending the email to the editor or signing up to speak at an event for your chosen profession. Notice the relief you feel when you take the next step. You may find yourself wondering why you took so long to get things started.

Step 3
Then, I want you to picture yourself doing the things that you are afraid of all the time. Are you able to see the type of person you would be, always putting yourself out there without receiving feedback, without going on the defensive, or going after your dreams without any restraint?

This is a pretty fun exercise until you do it. When these concepts are applied to our lives, things become very scary. So, what are you supposed to do? Start out small. Pick one thing that you have been avoiding and do it.

Mark Twain also said, "Eat a live frog first thing in the morning, and nothing worse will happen to you the rest of the day." Your job is to figure out what your frog is. This is your absolute worst-case scenario. Then I want you to swallow the frog.

What is it that will happen once your fears are realized? It is probably not going to be as bad as you have it in your head. Go ahead and do it. I'll wait. This will give you the chance to move on.

Did you ever play the game Red Rover as a child? You can probably hear those children screaming, "Red Rover, Red Rover, let Jane come over." You stood there, shaking, as Jane came running towards you. What did you choose to do? The only thing you thought you could do is to let go of your partner's hand. You quit. You didn't even try. And you likely felt regret after you did that.

Well, I'm giving you another chance to grab hold and not let go. The only difference is there is no threat of bodily harm. Grab up what you are afraid of and never let go. The worst thing that could happen is that you fail. You will write up something that is sub-par, or people won't understand your art. A critic may saunter along and tell you that he loathes your work. You will feel hurt.

The world will not end if you fail. It's something that everybody encounters as they work their way to success. So please, quit trying to accomplish things without fail. It's not going to work out for you. So, if you are serious about taking hold of your life, you need to learn how to fail.

Anything you do is going to take some practice. As said by Winston Churchill, "Success is stumbling from failure to failure with no loss of enthusiasm." What is it that is holding you back? It can't possibly be a failure.

Overcoming Failure

The one who failed many times are the ones that are highly successful. We tend to only know about their successes but not the struggles they went through to get to the success they currently have. We just compare ourselves to what they have achieved because we are not exposed to their mistakes and failures. This will only make it hard for us to accept the mistakes and problems that we will encounter. We are second guessing ourselves and question our skills. We don't realize that adversity is necessary to succeed.

This thinking is the reason why the world is so scared to fail. Even at a very young age, we are told that it is terrible to be wrong and make mistakes. Even our mind will use painful memories of what has happened in the past to cause negative emotions such as anxiety and fear to keep us from making similar errors today.

J.K. Rowling, an award-winning author, embraced her failures: "It is impossible to live without failing at something unless you live so cautiously that you might as well not have lived at all – in which case, you fail by default."

Diana Nyad, a swimmer, tried five times to swim from Cuba to Florida. Alfred Nobel ended up blowing up his lab, as well as his broth, in his eventually successful attempt to create dynamite, and then ended up funding the Nobel Prize. On a recent Google Hangout with National Geographic, a group of adventurers and scientist talked about all their failures. In every single case, no matter how wrong, frustrating, or depressing the events were, their failures taught them a lesson and allowed them to be able to move forward even if they had to take a different path. Being human means that we are going to fail often.

Most scientists are wrong most of the time, and almost all athletes will end up failing most of the time when they attempt a basket, goal, or a hit. The failure rate and the heartbreak that comes along with it is all part of our everyday life. Failures and setbacks are an inevitable part of life, nobody is perfect, and we all have our own hard times. Why is it that we end up taking failure so hard? Because, we often forget that success is only achieved through trying things repeatedly and trying will usually end in failure.

One could even argue that our ability to handle failure in creative ways is what has enabled the first humans to be able to navigate around and out of Africa hundreds of thousands of years ago. Think about the number of times that small groups of our human ancestors tried to come up with functional stone tools, wooden spears, or communicate complex topics to each other, and then ended up failing. It took our ancestors almost a million years to figure out how they could control fire, to hunt big animals, and then nearly three-quarters of a million more to find out that they could paint out their lives on the walls of caves. If you look at human history, you will see more failures than success, and this is an excellent thing.

The primary way to reach success is to achieve resilience when faced with failure and persevering when you are faced with adversity, and this has been a part of our evolution. Hannah Block wrote this for National Geographic, "...without the sting of failure to spur us to reassess and rethink, progress would be impossible."

Active imagination, hope, and dreams, despite facing severe challenges, are just a part of the reason why we, as humans, have done so well. When you fail at something, it shows you your limitations, and it will force you to reevaluate or rethink how you did things. Then, you will learn how to do those things better. It will add a roadblock, make you use your brain, and ups the ante. You then must cooperate and get a little creative with your world. This is the type of thing that humans do best. Unfortunately, our society tends to view failing as a flaw, or a failure of character, and that it is a problem that must be avoided.

Let's take a moment and think about science. The most common result of any experiment is failure. The most successful scientific discoveries are created by refuting the hypothesis, by showing that they were wrong and that their first attempts failed. It's how they analyze the failures' details and reconstitute their approach that will make them succeed more. Remember how the internet, antibiotics, or electric lights were developed. Every great success had antecedents that were rife with failures. How can we then train ourselves to use these challenges to our advantage? To turn your negative experiences into positive, follow the steps below.

Accept That Failure Is Going to Happen.
When we are going through something fierce, the most frustrating thing that we can be told is to "stay positive." Everybody has already abused, misconstrued, and misused the idea of positive thinking.

Smiling and being happy through all the things that happened have very little to do with all the things we hear. If somebody says that, they are either crazy or lying. Positive thinking is used to help us evolve, learn, and grow from the things that we experience.

This does not mean that you must try to fail. All of this says that when you face a setback, you must understand that it is not the end. This is just a step on the path where you're supposed to be. When you do have to go through difficulties, it is okay for you to feel down on yourself. It is perfectly reasonable to get disappointed and upset. Your goal should be to not stay feeling down.

Release Your Frustrations.

After you have given yourself and you have cleared your mind, you will then be able to accept the things that happened. That first emotional rush you experience will eventually dissipate, and then you will be able to slowly return your focus back to what you need to face.

Be Extremely Honest.

Take a few moments to reflect on what had happened and honestly tell yourself the reason why that situation occurred. Most people will do anything to avoid confronting their self with their own mistakes.

However, we will not learn anything if we don't take the time to do this. We may fail insanely if we don't learn from our mistakes. Albert Einstein famously explained that doing the same thing repeatedly and expecting a different result can be defined as insanity. If we can't learn from the failures and mistakes that we go through, then we will be doomed to continue repeating these mistakes.

Fail Forward.

Failing forward means that you have learned from your mistakes and adjusted it, so you succeed. Every change made, every person met, and every piece of data that you obtained is what is going to come together and give you the chance to make a different outcome.

There is no way to stop obstacles from happening, but you can learn how to handle them. They could end up blocking your vision momentarily, but if you persevere, you will find opportunities that have always been there for you that you just couldn't see. As you become more efficient with your process, you will be able to enable yourself to see that positive side of things in the hardest situations.

Not every failure will turn into success, and many are insurmountable, but that's not the point. It's our ability as humans to work our way towards goals, to hope, and to imagine the impossible that plays a vital role in the reason why we are still on this planet. The reason for human innovation is that we have hope, act on said hope, and can hold onto hope even when we are faced with a setback. So, when you end up failing, remember that you are in good company. Do what is human and get back up and try again.

Believe that you can accomplish this thing and that you are able to achieve your wildest dreams no matter what they are. If you feel stuck, find your frog and swallow it. If you end up failing, try it again. The critical thing to remember is that "can't" doesn't exist.

Chapter 5:
Developing Good Habit Fundamentals

Habits can shape our lives more than we even realize. Habits are incredibly strong. Our brains will cling to them and exclude all other things even common sense. Around 40 percent of everything we do every day is not decisions but habits we have formed.

Habits are important, and they get stronger with time and soon become second nature. You need to be sure you have the right kind of practices. Habits get their power from creating neurological cravings. When a behavior is performed, the body receives rewarded because the brain releases a pleasure chemical. Habits work on a loop:

- Trigger/cue: This could be a feeling, a person, specific time, or location
- Routine: This could be biting your nails, eating chocolate, smoking, or watching television
- Reward: Pleasure chemicals are released by the brain because of this routine.

This is a self-reinforcing mechanism that will become automatic with time. Once a habit is formed, the brain will stop participating in making decisions. Knowing how habits work on the loop will make it easier to gain control over them. When you can break down a habit into all its components, it makes it easier to change the logic of this loop. Habits get encoded into the structure of our brain and save us effort since we don't have to relearn all the things we do daily.

The Right Habits

Because our actions have become automatic, it gives us energy that we can use to focus on other tasks. This could be a good thing. If you begin to develop bad habits, you will need to interrupt it and make a new one. If you don't fight the bad habits consciously and replace them with new ones, this pattern you have created will happen automatically over, and over each time the habit gets triggered.

Your brain doesn't know the difference between good and bad habits. You must consciously decide that. You need to figure out what routines or actions you want to have and use the loop to help you. The only way to make positive changes is to turn your desired actions into habits. There is good news. Habits are not destiny. Habits can be replaced, changed or ignored. It isn't easy since habits won't ever really go away. They are only replaced by new ones.

Golden Rule

As stated above, habits won't disappear. You can't completely get rid of a bad one, you can only change it. Here is the way the Golden Rule works:

- Use the exact same trigger.
- Change up the routine.
- Give the exact same reward.

The Importance of Good Habits

- About half of the things you do daily are habits.
- Habits have power since they create neurological cravings.
- Habits work on a loop.
- Once a habit is created, the brain no longer participates in making decisions.
- Automatic actions give you the energy to be used doing other things.
- You absolutely must control your habits. Brains don't have the ability to know the difference between good and bad ones.
- Use the Golden Rule to make the correct changes.

Sleep

What you do during the day and right before you go to bed can impact your sleep. These can cause sleeplessness or promote healthy sleep. Daily routines such as what you drink and eat, how you spend your evenings, how your regular schedule plays out, and the medicines you must take can impact your sleep quality. Even a slight adjustment can mean the difference between having a sound sleep and restless nights. Writing in a sleep diary for two weeks can help you begin to understand how your routines are affecting your rest.

Sleep hygiene is healthy sleep habits that will improve your ability to go to sleep and remain asleep. These habits are the backbone of cognitive behavioral therapy. This is the most effective treatment for people who have chronic insomnia. Cognitive behavioral therapy helps address the behaviors and thoughts that keep us from sleeping. It also gives you techniques to help reduce stress, relax, and schedule a sleep routine. If you have problems sleeping and need improving your sleep, try to follow these healthy habits. Speak with your physician if your problems persist.

Quick Tips
You can use the tips to create some healthy sleep habits:

- Keep a constant schedule. At the same time each day including weekends and on vacations, you need to get up.

- Have a bedtime that gets you in bed early enough that you will get no less than seven hours of sleep.

- Never go to bed if you aren't sleepy.

- If after 20 minutes, you haven't fallen asleep, get up.

- Create a bedtime routine that is relaxing.

- Use the bed for only sex and sleep.

- Your bedroom needs to be relaxing and quiet. Keep the room at a cool but comfortable temperature.

- Limit the amount of time you are exposed to bright light during the evenings.

- Turn off all electronic devices 30 minutes before going to bed.

- Never eat large meals before bedtime. If you feel hungry, try eating a light snack that is healthy.

- Eat a healthy diet and get regular exercise.

- Don't drink caffeine during the late afternoon or evenings.

- Don't drink alcohol before going to bed.

- Don't drink a lot of fluids before you go to bed.

Diet

To maintain a healthy lifestyle, you need to create healthy eating habits and stick with them. Exercise is just 50 percent of the health equation. The other half is nutrition. If you don't have healthy eating habits, you aren't going to be able to have good fitness and health. What you eat does play a factoring role in your health and in this modern day of rushed schedules and convenience, it is effortless to eat things that aren't healthy. Here are some things to think about that will keep you on track.

Get Educated

You need to know what foods are healthy and the ones that aren't. You could talk to your doctor or a dietician to help you get started. Do some research on the web or find some books about nutrition. Most foods you get from fast food restaurants, or convenience stores are loaded with sugar, salt, and many other unhealthy ingredients. These ingredients are usually hidden, so you need to know how to read a food label.

Know what ingredients you need to stay away from. The main ingredients are always listed first. Look at and compare fat content because most foods that are promoted as low fat are most of the time very high in fat. Knowing what is in most foods will help you find the unhealthy one you might otherwise eat.

Substitute Ingredients and Foods

Back in the day, when someone wanted to eat healthily, it meant eating bland foods that had absolutely no taste. Remember when veggie burgers tasted like cardboard? Those days are behind us as technology has dramatically improved. Most of the low-fat versions of foods such as frozen yogurt and cheese taste as good as the full-fat versions.

You can also cook great tasting food by substituting some simple ingredients. Begin using olive oil instead of butter to fry. Lessen the amount of salt by adding spices. Find leaner cuts of meat and trim off any visible fat before you cook it. You could also cut back on eating red meat and eat more poultry and fish. Find some recipes that use chicken and fish. You will be amazed that you don't even miss red meat.

The most significant area to work on is your snacks. Don't reach for the potato chips and chocolate bars. Instead, reach for fruit or nuts. During hot summer days, freeze some grapes for a healthy, midday cooling snack.

Keep Your Goals in Mind
To help you stick with your healthy habits after you have created them, you need to keep your goals in mind. If your goal is maintaining those abs that you have worked hard to get, each time you look in the mirror, check their condition to make sure you continue to eat right.

You might also like to ski during the winter months. If you want to perform well on the slopes, keep this goal in mind to keep you fit all year long. Find other related activities that you would like to do well and relate them back to nutrition. When you follow these things in mind, you will be able to stay away from bad foods. You don't want to blame a bad performance on a bad diet.

Stay Around People Who Eat Healthily
You need to have people around you that will help you keep your goals. It is hard to eat right when everyone around you is eating unhealthily. Be sure you spend time with people who eat healthy, too. This will inspire you to keep eating healthy. You are using teamwork to help you get to your goal of eating healthy.

There isn't a magic potion on how to create healthy eating habits and making them stick. Having good health is a life-long commitment, and the easiest way to achieve it is by all the little goals you have reached when you eat a healthy meal and complete another exercise routine. If you can follow these tips, you will eventually have optimum health.

Exercise
The biggest problem with trying to create a habit of exercising is that you try to do it three or four times every week and this just makes it too hard. The

reason behind this is the more constant an action is, there is a more likelihood of it becoming a habit.

Exercising daily will more than likely result in a habit. It will become automatic and more natural instead of always struggling with it. You can implement this into your daily life, too. You can alternate different exercises each day like strength training, biking, swimming or running. You might have a goal of competing in a marathon. The only way of doing this is to make running a daily habit. If you are dedicated to making this a habit, here are some tips that will help you make exercise a daily practice:

Pick a specific time. Figure out a time that you will stick with whether it be during the evening, lunchtime or mornings. You must stick with this time. If you don't choose a specific time, you might put it off until the next day or when you have more energy or time. Soon, this will never be a habit at all.

Send reminders to yourself. Many apps will send you reminders either by text or email. This way, you won't ever forget. When you get the reminder, do it right then. Don't delay.

Begin small. This is the most useful of the suggestions. When you begin exercising, you will have massive amounts of energy, ambition, and enthusiasm. You will think you can do more than you can. Doing too much at first could lead to burnout, and this will lead to stopping your habit. When you just begin making exercise a daily habit, your body isn't going to be used to dealing with the stress you are putting on it. The main thing is to only do about 20 minutes when you begin. Take is easy. Don't do anything hard. Even doing 10 to 15 minutes is better than nothing. The key is getting out there. Slowly get your body used to exercising daily and create that habit.

Progress later. When your body is finally used to exercising daily, you can slowly begin to increase the intensity and amount of your exercises. Wait about two weeks before starting an increase. This is the minimum that your body needs to get adjusted. When it begins to feel too easy, this is the time to increase the length of your routines to 30 or 40 minutes. You will eventually be about to do it for an hour. When you can work out for an hour, and it feels relatively easy, begin increasing the intensity, like running harder or faster. Try not to increase both strength and distance at the same time.

Make it fun. If you connect a habit with pain, you won't do it. If it is fun, you will want to do it. When you are beginning an exercise routine, the more fun it is, the more you will be willing to do it. If you are running, go slow at first; enjoy the scenery, fresh air, beautiful skies, the solitude, the sun rises or sets, and contemplation. Make it something you enjoy doing. Listening to music helps, too.

Lay out the gear. If your new habit doesn't create any friction and doesn't have any obstacles, it will be more of a success. If you are getting up early to run, you don't want to have to gather up all your gear when you are still half asleep. You may just crawl back into bed. If you lay out your clothing, shoes, mp3 player, and watch, you will be ready to head out the door in no time at all without having to face obstacles.

Get out the door. Plan to get your shoes on and get out the door. Don't worry about how long the run is going to be or how hard it might be. Just get out the door and get it started. Once you are out the door, the rest is a piece of cake.

Mix it up. When you mix things up, you will have a variety of activities to do. This makes things more interesting. It is just as important that with each exercise, you are training different muscles, especially if you are swimming. Some muscles are being constantly used, but they get used differently with different stresses being put on them. What this means is that you aren't pounding the same muscles each day. This gives them the time to recover. If you don't let them heal, you will break your muscles down with time.

Have a day of rest. Recovery is significant. Therefore, you should let your body rest. If you are going slow and just doing 20 minutes, you are going to be fine without having rest days. It is still good to have a day of rest. A day where you aren't doing the exercises, you do the other days. You don't ever want to skip a day entirely since you won't be consistent with the habit. Try doing a day of strength training. You won't be using the same muscles as you are the other six days. If your muscles need more rest, you could just try to do a day of walking or try meditation. The main point is to do something each day that will keep your habit going.

Never skip a day. It is easy to train for five days then tell yourself you've been good, and you deserve a down day. This will make forming this habit harder. Being constant is the key. Try not to skip a day. If you do, you don't have to beat yourself up about it. Never judge. Never feel bad. Everybody slips up every now and then. Forming habits is a skill that takes practice. Just start it back the next day and find the obstacle that caused you to skip a day. Be prepared for it this time.

Chapter 6:
Vocabulary for Success

Many people will use phrases like: "I wish I could," "I don't know how," "I can't," and "I won't" in their everyday talk. It is fine to use these words if the situation demands it. People who use these self-limiting lingos regularly are subconsciously tunneling themselves into a life of self-doubt, powerlessness, and limitations. In other words, somebody that uses phrases like: "This is going to be mine," "I am," and "I can" will attract abundance, success, and achievement just because this type of language puts them into the right frame of mind to succeed.

When you constantly use phrases like the above, you will end up feeling miserable, victimized, and anguished even if you did your best in these situations.

When you work through your problems by thinking you can, you achieved great results even if you didn't have the best solution when you began. You believed you could and found a way to work through the problems.

What category do you fall under? Do you use self-doubting and negative lingo daily? How do you begin using language that empowers such as "I will," "I can,"

"I will get it finished?" You just need to replace that negative lingo with the empowering lingo.

While working on your language, remember that language can affect a person's self-confidence instead of being the cause. Build your self-confidence and self-belief at the same time. You might be in a meeting and immediately felt the vibe in the room change just because someone said something.

Words are powerful. Even one word can change how others see you, set your boundaries, put you out, and win you over. With this type of power, it is best to understand the psychology and science of words. Here are the top ten phrases and words that will motivate us:

If: Describes A Positive Hypothetical; Improves Performance

Here is a universal truth. Nobody likes to be wrong, especially if you are in front of other people. When you face many "I don't know" during a tough challenge or brainstorming session, the small word "if" could alleviate the pressure of being wrong and open a path to critical thinking. Here is a specific sentence that you should use a lot: "What would you say if you did know?"

By using the little word "if," it lets others you are talking to think hypothetically. This takes all the pressure away that prevents them from answering. When you can describe a hypothetical outcome positively, it will increase their expectation for success and improves their performance. The key is the hypothetical element and it needs to be triggered by "if".

Could: Use This in Place of Should to Get Creative
Magic also happens when you use the word "could" especially if you substitute it for the word "should." These two words sound very similar, but research shows us that "should" will narrow a person's field of vision and will limit potential answers. The word "could" will open a person's mind to new possibilities.

When talking about ethical dilemmas, shifting your mindset from "What should I do?" to "What could I do?" will generate a moral insight. This is defined as realizing that competing values aren't incompatible. You can change to a new train of thought just by choosing a different word.

Yes: Three Yeses Can Close A Deal
Yes, is another small magic word. It is very interesting to see how one yes can lead to another. One study looked at the possibility that getting someone to say yes while conversing would affect the entire outcome of the conversation. First, a salesperson did business as usual and was able to close about 18 percent of the sales. They were then instructed to get the customers to say yes three times early in the conversation. Suddenly, they were closing on 32 percent of

the sales. Tiny yeses can be any type of affirmative such as responding to a question such as "You are here for the four o'clock appointment, right?"

Together: Will Make Teams Work Smarter and Harder

The word together is about interconnectivity, belonging, and relatedness. This is powerful things for our brains because belonging is very elemental to our hierarchy of needs. It isn't surprising that using the word "together" can help people become more efficient.

Participant worked on hard puzzles by themselves. One group was told they would work together and would receive tips from other members. The group who heard "together" had astounding results. These people:

- Had better recall on what they saw.
- Worked almost 50 percent longer.
- Said the puzzle was more interesting.
- Solved problems correctly.
- Said they weren't as tired by the task.

The word together will motivate you to feel like you are part of something larger than yourself. Words like "we" and "let's" can build a sense of togetherness and connection.

Thank You: Makes People Likely to Seek Out Relationships

Gratitude not only makes our lives happier, but it can also help you further your career and relationships. Research shows that when you thank someone for their help, it makes them want to seek out an ongoing relationship with you.

One study of students that provided advice to young students showed that only a few were thanked for their help. The ones who were thanked provided their contact details when asked for it like their email address or phone number. The students who said "thank you" were also said to have warmer personalities. When you say, "thank you", it shows others that you are a person they can have a quality relationship with. There are five elements to an effective thank you:

- Compliment the benefactor's attributes
- Recognize the benefactor's costs
- Be timely
- Recognize the benefactor's intent
- Articulate the benefits

Choose To: Use Instead Of "Have To"

Completing an exercise that is called "have to" to "choose to" can change your life in a huge way.

Step One: What happens in your life that you don't think is playful? Write out on a piece of paper all the things that you must do. List all activities that you don't like but do because you think you don't have a choice.

Step Two: After you have finished your list, clearly define all the things you do just because you choose to, not because you must. Insert words like "I choose to…" in front of everything you have listed.

Step Three: After you have acknowledged that you have chosen to do a certain activity, find out the intention behind your choice by completing this statement, "I choose to… because I want …"

And: This Is the Best Way to Put A Contrary Opinion

If you need to disagree with somebody, express your opinion as an "and." It isn't necessary for another person to be wrong and for you to be right. When you are surprised to hear what the other person has said, don't interrupt with "That isn't right!" You only must add your perspective. Say this instead: "You are saying we need to keep room in the budget for the event, and I am worried about money for the employees to be trained. Do we have any options?" Here are some other phrases that will help you be heard:

- "I came to this conclusion because…"
- "Do you see any flaws with my reasoning?"

- "I would love to hear your reactions to what I said."

- "Here is what I am thinking."

- "Do you see the situation differently?"

- "My perspective is based on the following assumptions..."

Because: This Word Can Make You Feel Rational and Objective

One of the two very important words in blogging is also a top one for motivating people: Because. Ellen Langer, a social psychologist, tested this word by asking people to get in front of them in line at a copy place. She used three different variations:

- "Excuse me, I have five pages. May I use the copy machine?"

- "Excuse me, I have five pages. May I use the copy machine because I am in a hurry?"

- "Excuse me, I have five pages. May I use the copy machine because I have to make some copies?"

Around 60 percent of the people she asked allow her in front of them when she used the first technique. When she added the 'because', one rated at 93 percent and the other at 94 percent. When you would like people to act, you need to give them a reason. When you use cause and effect reasoning, it works because it makes your request sound rational and objective instead of subjective and biased. Here is a list of cause and effect phrases:

- Thus
- Therefore
- Since
- For this reason
- Due to
- Consequently
- Caused by
- As a result
- Accordingly

You could take this a step further with what is called the Advanced Because Technique. The idea behind this is to get you to say because to yourself. Instead of giving another person thousands of reasons to try something, ask them "Why?" Once you can do that, they will figure out their own because. It is now their reasons, and no longer your problem.

Other's Names: We Like Things That Are Connected to Us

Virginia has 30 percent more people that are named Virginia than any other state. Louisiana has 37 percent more people named Louis than any other state. Georgia has 88 percent Georgia's than any other state.

This is called the Name-Letter Effect. This is a weird phenomenon that shows most people possess associations about themselves and prefer things that connect to that self. A person's name is the most important and sweetest sound in any language. There is evidence that certain brain patterns can happen when we hear our names as opposed to hearing other people's names.

Willing: This Could Turn A "No" Into A "Yes"

While answering hundreds of calls between potential clients and mediators, Elizabeth Stoke discovered a magic word that changed minds: "Willing." Most callers were ready to reject mediation because they thought the other party was a person who wouldn't mediate.

When the mediator asked a person if they were "willing" to mediate, even the most resistant caller agreed to try their service. "Willing" was more effective than any other phrase like "you might be interested in mediation." "Willing" was the only word that changed a no to a yes. This works because if one party is a person who won't mediate, then the person calling will be. Here is a list of words you need to stop using immediately:

- Fast
- Just
- Easy
- Can't
- Must
- Need
- Ugly
- Not enough
- Stupid
- Never
- Busy

More importantly these negative words are the true heavy hitters that should not be used:

Only. This one works with the word "just," too. You might have caught yourself using the word only such as "I only walked five miles today." "I'm emailing you just to tell you...", "I just started yoga today." It is time to stop doing that. Stay away from thinking about any day as a test to your character. It doesn't matter if you ran three blocks or three miles. Today isn't about you personally. Take each day as a day to progress a little farther. People that approach goals and challenges with a mindset of growing instead of as a test won't see any setbacks as failures but opportunities to learn better habits and develop better skills. If you don't run as far as you wanted, it is fine. Tomorrow is another day, and you will do it then.

Fat: This word works along with "ugly." Women are very guilty of telling themselves they are ugly. It is human nature to self-depreciate. To be able to form more accurate and better self-images, you must get rid of all negative adjectives. Stop yourself from using self-defeating talk and make conscious choices to change. You aren't fat, you are getting healthy. You might not believe this at first, but if you can learn to use positive language, you will soon talk yourself into thinking it.

Too much: This one goes with the phrase above, too. It is easy to think we are too much wrong or not enough right. This just reinforces all the embedded presupposition factors in the brain. If you were to ask yourself, "Why aren't I enough?" your brain will immediately begin looking for answers. It acts as an internet search. You will find what you are looking for eventually. Instead of assuming you aren't good enough, think about affirmations. These will reframe the questions that lead your mind to search for answers and stay away from the endless repetition of the common affirmations. Ask yourself: "Why am I enough?" When you do this, you are setting your brain on the correct path, and you might be delightfully surprised with what your mind comes up with.

Won't: This word works along with the word can't. When you tell yourself that you can't eat a hamburger or you won't lose weight when you don't work out, this is working against you. When trying to make change happen, you must avoid negative language. You need to fill your mind with definite ideas. If you don't, you are going to confuse it with unfavorable terms. The brain will drop the won't or can't and will focus on what you would like to do. Many times, all those won't or can't statements just aren't true. Try to focus on what you will and can do. Tell yourself things such as: "I can have a cheat meal today," "There are a lot of delicious and healthy snacks that will keep me full," "I will lose weight because I am working out each day." There is only one exception to this rule, and that is your physical limitations. If you can't eat a food because of food allergies or workout due to a physical handicap or injury, your mind might remind you to protect itself. Try to keep your eyes on what you can do instead of what you can't.

Failure: When you call yourself a failure, this is the best way to make yourself fail at everything you try. You are fulfilling your own self-prophecy. You need to be the best positive coach you can be to yourself. When you do that, you take "I'm not good" and change it into "I am good, and I can do this"; or "I'm a failure" into "I have failed but also won, I will win this time, too." You also don't want to lie to yourself. You need to make room for disappointments. If you expect perfection, you are going to fail. You must forgive yourself, be patient with changing and let yourself grow.

Lucky: There are going to be days that you feel fortunate, and that is wonderful. You shouldn't use luck as a reason for why you can't do something or to discredit somebody else. You can have luck, but it must be used with hard work to accomplish things. Don't compare your life with other people's lives. While you envy somebody's legs, arms, or abs, don't ever say they are lucky. Tell yourself that they worked hard to get the body they have, and you can have the same rock-hard abs if you work hard at it, too.

Tomorrow: If you consistently put things off until another day, you are never going to get them done. One common trap is saying, "I didn't eat right today, so I'll start my diet tomorrow." This lets you keep delaying it, and it will never really start. Try to pick a realistic and concrete begin date and stick with it. You must make yourself accountable. If you aren't going to do it tomorrow, when are you doing to do it? You also need to have a reason behind the diet to stay motivated. You need to know "why" and not just "how." It doesn't matter if you are trying to lower your blood pressure, stop smoking, and the risk of diabetes. You are setting an excellent example for your children. You might want to get fit so you can look great in your swimsuit next summer, choose a reason and remind yourself daily.

Stephen Patterson

When you are working with others, be careful of using the above words. Watch out when you use them. Watch out when you hear them. These could really get you in trouble.

Chapter 7:
Strategies for Self-Discipline

We aren't born having self-discipline. It is something we develop with time. It is much like strengthening our muscles. To start creating self-discipline, you need certain factors to happen. Some of these things will come from inside you and others will come from external sources. Let's explore some of these factors.

You Need A Why

To develop self-discipline, you need to have a desire to reach a goal. Without this desire, there isn't much hope in having self-discipline.

Self-discipline requires fuel, and this comes from either motivation or inspiration. You need one of the two to give ammunition to your self-discipline. If not, you might struggle to remain focused over long time periods. This basically boils down to having enough reasons to undertake every task you commit to doing. You need to ask yourself these questions:

- What exactly is it that I want?
- Why do I desire this?

- What do I need to do specifically to get this done?

- The better the reasons you can identify, the more fuel you must drive forward your self-discipline.

Unmoving Accountability and Commitment

Reasons aren't enough. You need the commitment to do whatever is required to get to your goal. It isn't ever easy. Long-term commitment does take discipline, and typically, this isn't something that many people are good at. Most people just lack some accountability. Long-term commitments require we hold ourselves accountable or have somebody else hold us accountable. Both methods will work. If they can work together, this is when you will get the best results.

Requires Rewards and Penalties

Levels of motivation can come and go as we move forward toward our goals. There will be a time when we feel very motivated and others we might struggle to get through certain activities or tasks during out day.

To stop falling into these cycles, it would be helpful to implement some rewards and penalties. Awards and punishments could be used to direct your behavior through the day.

You can give yourself a reward for making certain choices of acting a certain way. You could also penalize yourself for engaging in harmful behaviors or making bad decisions. These rewards and penalties add another element to your internal desires that keep the fire of self-discipline burning bright during your day.

Personal Standards

If there is any lack of self-discipline in any parts of your life, it is because you don't hold yourself accountable for keeping certain standards. These standards you keep will keep you on target while you are working toward your goal. These are unspoken rules that will guide your actions, behavior, decisions, and choices through your day. Keep that in mind while we outline some standards you should uphold while pursuing your goals. Ask yourself these questions:

- If I get off track, how can I correct things?
- Are there any choices and behaviors I will not tolerate?
- Are there any choices and behaviors that I will accept?
- What standards am I going to uphold?

This basically comes down to making an agreement with yourself. Knowing what you will or won't accept are the basics for self-discipline. You will then have to keep yourself accountable for following through on these agreements. You must regulate and correct your behavior when you get off track. This is what self-discipline is about. There is one more point we still need to talk about. That is the environment.

Competitive Environment
The last layer requires you to make a competitive environment that will drive you toward your goal. This isn't saying you are competing with other people. You can place yourself into a frame of mind where you try to outperform and outwork others. This is one way to discipline yourself. There is one other way to do this, too. You need to compete against your best self. You need to measure your current results against your past performance and can be useful when helping you stay disciplined, motivated, and focused. It might just be the main ingredient that fuels your self-discipline when things don't go your way.

Chapter 8:
Controlling Your Environment

Many people think that intentions are followed by habits. Truthfully, the primary purpose of the brain is to look for patterns and use it as shortcuts so it can process all the information, we receive every day. We rely on environmental triggers more than we think we do. Researchers have found that students who transferred to a new school changed their habits. It is observed that if they were not exposed to normal cues, it is much easier for them to break the habit.

The example above proves the research conducted with regards to the stimulus control theory. The effect of the stimulus on behavior can be described by the example. These techniques can even be used to help insomnia patients. People who have problems fallings asleep were told to just lie down on their bed if they were tired. If they still can't fall asleep, they can go and try in a different room.

This advice may be strange, but eventually, researchers saw that by connecting bed with "time to sleep" and not any other activities like watching television or reading, subjects were able to fall asleep because this process is repeated.

Since the trigger has been created, it becomes automatic to fall asleep when they head to bed. Maybe we are like Pavlov's dog after all. Finding out how our behavior can be impacted by just little cues can somehow be scary. Eating with a large spoon will make you eat more. Chewing on a big plate will make you eat more. You won't eat as much chocolate if you move it away from your desk.

- Good behavior can be encouraged by these triggers.

Change your behavior using your environment. Just like how muscles can be worn out, discipline also does as well. You can use environmental changes to help you do hard tasks. Here are some methods to help you develop this:

Task Association
To be able to write well, you must be able to read well. When you write on the internet, this can become a problem since you can quickly turn on your next inspiration.

One method that you can use is to set up specific devices to do specific activities. Your office needs to be designated to only a workspace. Don't fill the room or space with fun things to do. You can also choose a location outside your home. These are sometimes more effective. You can go to a library or a coffee shop if you have some writings to do which will become associated with the time to write.

Increase or Reduce Friction

Making specific tasks harder or easier to can be affected by the environment. If your goals cannot guide you to make behaviors easier, it can be harmful. Instead of focusing on doing an individual behavior, it is much better to focus on making the action easier instead. You need to get rid of times when you just want to give up. You can make these moments more intense if you're going to prevent yourself from making a bad habit.

Habits are a way to simplify movements that are needed to get a particular result. Increasing friction is an excellent way to influence your behavior. Since willpower is fragile, focus your energies on making hard habits harder to do. If you want to reduce friction, the best example is the "hit the ground running" with your most healthy habit.

If you have a hard time getting out the door every morning, put your gym clothes in your bag and place it by the door. Put your purse and jacket on the counter next to the door. When you have high willpower, get rid of any excuse. Don't force habits. Take some effort and make good habits easier to do and bad habits harder to engage with.

Use Contextual Cues

It is easier to build a constant habit when you create it off an existing one. To simplify, one task will get more natural if it is either followed or preceded by another job you enjoy. Since the second task happens at every day at the same time, it is easy to build on top of it since there is a trigger you can rely on each day. Try to schedule tasks during constant times of your schedule like after or during lunch, when you wake up, as soon as you get home.

Have Routines

Things don't always happen in one night. Performing the same habit repeatedly can result in success. Research has found that having too many choices is the long-term goal's enemy. Having a lot of options makes consistent behavior harder to do. You need to practice making routines out of the essential aspects of your life to maintain consistency. You can be aggressive in other parts of your life.

A good example is the average spending versus saving don't rely on willpower alone to save money. Take this decision away by having withdrawals taken out of our paycheck into a savings account. This will let you worry less about spending since the banking system has taken care of this for you by getting rid of the money before you have a chance to see it. This small change can have an impact since it will compound if you do it right. Find the areas in your life that you think are mundane, and then make a routine out of these aspects when you can. Try to make fewer decisions.

Chapter 9:
Develop Drive

It is normal to need a boost after you have worked all day. Motivators such as praise and money will only get you so far. They might kickstart your journey, but they won't get you to the finish line. You are going to need a strong inner drive when obstacles get in your way. Here are some ways to strengthen your internal drive:

Journal
This one might take some work to become a habit, but it will be totally worth it. Journaling won't just document your journey; it is a way for you to get rid of all your feelings and thoughts so you can focus on what matters. Write down your goals, list things you are grateful for, record what you did during the week. Had a hard day at work? Write it down. Did something happen to inspire you? Write it down. After you have written in a journal for a while, you will realize you have a clearer head. You can even go back through to reminisce later.

Get Involved in The Community

It might be professional or personal but being a part of your community is a wonderful way to get your inner drive going. A group of people who are all working for a common goal will keep you motivated when you slip up. A community that is supportive makes you excited to go to work. Networking events, groups, co-working spaces, or online forums can be a great help when you need some motivation. If you want to work on the personal end of your drive, community centers, mentors, and local meetups are great places to begin.

Educate Other People

When you take the time to help educate people, it has a lot of personal benefits. You might not realize how much you know until you teach it to somebody else. This can boost your confidence. When educating others, it might be one person or a whole workshop; you are saying that you are successful and a reliable source of wisdom.

People will seek you out if they have a question about your expertise. That should give you enough motivation to hone your skills and work toward your goals. It is great to realize you have gone far enough to be able to teach others how to succeed the way you have. You must continually push yourself a bit harder to maintain this status.

Visualize Success

What is it going to look like when you finally reach your goals? Will you be taking the vacation of your dreams? You must look past the material rewards and focus on social and personal. Is it going to give you more family time every week? Will you be the main speaker at next year's conference?

Many people who can envision success can motivate them to push them toward their goals. Other people can make their conceptions concrete by creating a vision board. You can make this with a corkboard, some notebook paper or on Pinterest. Try to find pictures that show your idea of success. It might be images of a beach or photos of the family. If you can keep your vision board where you can see it, you will be reminded of why you must keep pushing forward, even when things get hard.

Practice Optimism

To quote Henry Ford: "Whether you think you can, or you think you can't, you're right." You might have seen this quote many times, and it still holds true. Your attitude is your primary ability to reach your goals. You can maintain a positive manner by using optimism during the day. Don't think you are bad at something; just tell yourself you are working on it. Don't focus on how much you hate doing something; look forward to things that excite you.

Stephen Patterson

Optimism isn't going to lead to success. You are still going to have to find resources and put in some effort. It will help you get there. When you feel like you are losing steam, a strong inner drive keeps you moving forward.

Chapter 10:
Directing Your Attention

A wise man gave his protégé this riddle to solve: "You possess a potent tool – one that is always with you. You could use this tool any time to make decisions more efficiently, to make interactions with others more rewarding, and to find more joy in life. What is this amazing tool?"

This man studied a lot for years but couldn't solve this riddle. He was sitting on a bus one day and saw a couple in the seat next to him. The woman was talking to the man she was sitting with, the man wasn't listening as he was reading the newspaper. The girl seated in front of him was listening to her iPod while sending text messages. This man almost solved this riddle when he heard a noise and looked outside. He then realized he should have gotten off the bus two stops earlier. He had not been paying attention.

Attention and the ability to focus on it is the most powerful skill that we own. Many of us go through life without paying any attention to notice. That can cost us a lot. We could lose the ability to participate now. We may think we save time when we plan our meals while our partner talks about their day. What we are doing is robbing our partners and ourselves of the opportunity to connect deeper and be intimate.

Paying attention to just one thing at a time can give us many rewards including more joy out of life, more satisfying personal interactions, and decreased anxiety. Paying attention does take some practice, but it is a needed skill and one that is worth honing.

Attention Deficit

Think about attention as a flashlight. When you use it in the best way, we can light up a single object and be able to see it clearly. Focusing our attention this way is a lot easier said than done.

The hard part is trying to keep the flashlight focused on just one thing at a time through circumstance and hardwiring. Our brains are multifaceted and complex. They can engage in more than one thing at a time. In this high demand, fast-paced world, it usually comes with undesirable consequences and hidden costs.

One thing we always attempt involves focusing our attention on an internal and external stimulant at the same time. We might be trying to listen to our best friend tell about her breakup while going through the pantry in your mind trying to figure out what you are going to make for supper.

This usually doesn't work too well. When our attention gets split like this, we miss a lot of things that come at us. The more substantial cost might manifest itself in the form of emotional stress. Self-focused attention creates an endless loop where we think about what we are thinking about. This cycle tends to bring on worry and anxiety.

People that suffer from social anxiety like the fear of speaking in public focus on their own internal negative assumptions about certain situations instead of the world around us. This can lead to stress that distorts our view of our public interaction and performance. This, in turn, creates even more anxiety.

Many psychologists and psychiatrists believe emotional distress happens when we focus on ourselves too much. When we only focus inward, we can see the beauty around us. We suffer since our attention will pull us toward either the past or future instead of letting us stay in the present. This leads to feeling distressed like anxiety, food cravings, depression, and shyness.

Training Our Focus

To develop being able to focus our attention, we must overcome some obstacles. Being preoccupied is a significant enemy of focused attention. Another one is passive entertainment. Television moving at fast paces trains our brains to lose interest in things that don't move at high rates of speed. Multitasking is another thing that is hard to stay away from. Having a multitasking mind isn't efficient. It will rob you of being fully immersed in any activity.

Realizing these obstacles would be the first step to help sharpen our attention skills. You need to know where your focus is at. You could use an alarm on your watch to help you with that. You could set it to signal every 45 minutes. When you hear the alarm, you would stop and take notice of what you are doing. If you are worried about bills, or what a coworker said earlier in the day, you aren't paying attention to what is happening right now. Here are some strategies to help you shift your attention:

- Use large muscles. Go for a job or play handball.
- Begin a non-repetitive activity like gardening or cooking.
- Pick a fast-paced activity instead of a slow one. Go skiing instead of reading a book.

Activities that focus your mind and move your body will help shift your attention. You are going to find psychological relief, be in the moment, and find joy in everything you do.

Activities that focus your mind and move your body will help shift your attention. You are going to find psychological relief, be in the moment, and find joy in everything you do.

When you invest in developing your attention skills, you will be bettering every aspect of your life. The world comes alive when you can pay attention to it. There's no better time like the present to begin. You can master your attention skill by practicing. Here are two exercises to help you with this skill:

Do Only One Thing. Multitasking is typical for many people, but would your life fall apart if you stopped trying to do everything? Just experiment and see. Take a day and focus on just doing one thing at a time. When you are watching the news, just sit and watch the news. When you are talking to your best friend on the phone, give them your undivided attention to them. When you are eating, just eat. Turn off the television, put down the magazine, and turn off the computer. You might be surprised how great experiences can be when you give them your undivided attention.

Get Blue. Look for blue for an entire day. Actively scan for blue. From the smallest speck on a movie poster to the enormous expanse of sky. Make blue the focus of a mental treasure hunt that you will win all day.

Stephen Patterson

Chapter 11:
Social Motivation

Social motives can be defined as complex motive states. These get classified as social since they are learned in social groups such as families. They are also called secondary or learned motives. There are various social motives. We are going to look at the four most common reasons. These are:

Need for Achievement
This one is the most important of all. It's mainly concerned with setting goals and then achieving them. It wants to be successful in whatever it does. It wants to always avoid failing. People who have powerful achievement motives don't just want to be better than others but try to do better than they have done in the past.

People who have this high need to achieve will do better in school, their jobs, and all areas of their life. People will choose tasks that are not too easy or difficult but ones that they are confident they can accomplish with doing their best. The need to achieve can be influenced by these factors:

Trained to Be Independent as A Child
People who have the need for achievement usually come from families that have taught them to be independent since their childhood. Some are even given the freedom to do what they want to do.

Socio-Cultural Environment
This can also be a factor for having the need for achievement. In certain societies such as the Zuni Indians and the Arapesh of New Guinea, this is not a factor for them. The average American is in extreme need for achievement when compared to the average Indian.

Success from The Past
People who have a history of success in a task also have a high need for achievement when compared to people that have a history of failure.

Sex
This doesn't seem probable, but this can also influence a person's need for achievement. Women usually have lower requirements for performance when compared to men. Many women will suppress their need for achievement out of fear of success since success in the traditional text doesn't always bring social progress.

There has been a lot of work done on the need for achievement. This is related to economic growth. Societies who have a need for achievement also have a higher rate of economic growth as compared to communities who don't have a need for success.

Tests have been created to measure the need for achievement and social motives. Projective tests are what is generally used as the measurement for the need for success. One test is called the Thematic Apperception Test or TAT. Here are some characteristics of people who have a high need for achievement:

People who have a need for a result like working on challenging tasks that will get them success. They don't work on easy tasks where they aren't being tested because it isn't giving them any achievement. They also don't like functions that are extremely hard as they might fail at something.

- They like tasks where their performance gets compared to others. They love having feedback on how they are doing.

- They like working on things that are related to their career or that reflect their personal characteristics like intelligence. All this helps them to get ahead.

- When these people are successful, they will raise their expectations to a point where they can move on to a bit more difficult and challenging tasks.

- These people like to work in situations where they have control over its outcome. They aren't gamblers, though.

Power Motivation or Need for Power

The need for power is defined as the need to charm, lead, persuade, cajole, control, or influence others and to better their reputation with others. People who have a strong need for power get satisfaction from reaching their goals.

The need for power can be expressed in several ways: the degree of what the person fears about their own need for control, how mature they are, sex, and their socio-economic status. Here are some ways that people who have a need for power express themselves:

- Aggressive and impulsive actions.
- Playing competitive sports like swimming, boxing, football, hockey, etc.
- Joining an organization and then holding an office in that organization.
- With men: sexually dominating women and drinking.
- By obtaining possessions like a lot of credit cards, huge stereo equipment, guns, fancy cars, etc.
- Being around people who aren't very popular and who might be easy to control.

- Choosing careers like clergy, business owners, diplomacy, and teaching where they will be able to impact others.

- Disciplining and building their bodies. This holds very true for women who have a very strong need for power.

The concept of Machiavellianism is related to the need for power. This term was coined by psychologists to describe people that express their motivation to exploit and manipulate others in dishonest and deceptive ways.

Human Aggression

This can be defined as any behavior that is directed to a goal of injuring or harming another being who is trying to stay away from this treatment. Aggression could be indirect or direct, passive or active, verbal or physical.

There have been many theories about aggression. One popular approach to aggression is that it's instinctive in nature. Some researchers believe that aggression is the result of social and environmental factors. Aggression could have been caused by many social and environmental factors. Some of these are:

- Negative evaluation or verbal insult from other people.

- Being obedient to authority.

- Intense noise and crowding.

- Aggression is thought to be a learned behavior and is learned by many different learning principles.

Need for Affiliation

This common social motive relates to maintaining and expressing attitudes of loyalty to friends and family, winning other's affections, pleasing others, and interacting with peers.

Chapter 12: Measuring Progress

Being able to measure your progress is reasonable for many people. It isn't normal to be able to measure progress well. This can lead to misjudgments. You need to think about your progress more and make them a constant source for good.

Measuring can tell you how you are doing and the progress you have made. Checking on progress can help get you motivated. It can help you know if you have been slacking and will tell you if you need to change your course.

If you aren't thinking about the way you measure your progress, you might be measuring the wrong things or measuring it the wrong way. You could debilitate it or fall behind on a project or even miss out on opportunities. If you measure progress, you must do it right. Turn off the automatic gut and measure your progress mindfully.

Measure Your Process Goals

If you are a Type A person, you have probably overworked yourself, thinking that working more will give you more progress. Will it? Have you taken the time to measure? Just because you are stressed and overworked doesn't mean you are getting anything accomplished. You must figure out how far you are from your goal and if you are closing the gap.

You need to figure out what goals you are chasing. You need to know the difference between process and outcome goals. Outcome goals, such as wanting a promotion, are something you can strive to get. It isn't anything that you can do. Process goals are actions that can be measured. These could help you get closer to the outcome goal.

You need to measure your progress daily by moving toward your process goals. How much you work doesn't matter. What matters is the work that will take you closer to reaching your daily process goal. After that, you need to check to see if your process goals are doing what they are supposed to do and that is keeping track of your movements toward your outcome goal.

Let's say you work in sales and you need to make 30 cold calls every day. If you only send email, you can't count this as progress. If your outcome goal is to close sales, and you haven't locked any in a long time, you need to rethink your process goals. The number of calls isn't leading to sales. You need to make more progress on the quality of these calls. Make a new process goal by tweaking your sales pitch and work toward that.

Measure the Distance You Have Come

A different way to track your progress is by looking at how far you are from the starting point. Carl is a 24-year-old who has begun a possibly successful online company. His vision is to be the next Amazon.com. Yes, that seems impossible or at least many years away. Knowing he hasn't become Amazon yet is not a way to measure for progress. It is far enough in the future that you can't see what path is going to lead to his result.

Carl should concentrate on what he has accomplished so far. He started off sitting at his dining room table. Now he has his own office space. He has customers. He has a business that works. There is money in his bank account, and he is pulling in a profit. He needs to measure his progress on how far he has come and not on how far he must go. Carl can see his has made a lot of momentum and can be sure it will continue to unfold as more milestones get added to his list.

Measuring the Distance to Your Goal

There will come the point where your goal is going to be within your reach. At this point, you can begin to measure how far you are away from reaching that goal. You can now concentrate on getting that gap closed.

Be careful and don't do this too soon. You could hurt your morale. If you continuously ask yourself if you are there yet, you could give your soul a burst of inadequacy. When you are in a marathon, you get a surge of energy when you realize you are just a few feet from finishing. You see a large barrel of ice cream waiting for you at the finish line. Before you know it, you are bursting across the finish line. Once you have reached the halfway mark, begin to measure your progress by how fast you are achieving your goal. Keep that barrel of ice cream in mind and make new goals to push you those last few feet.

A great way to do this is to create a checklist of what you must do to reach this goal. These can be things like running tests with focus groups or writing an email asking for participants. When you have your plan on paper, finishing this project might seem a bit more doable because the steps you need are right in front of you. Even if you do some things wrong, just plan to get you energized and motivated.

Measure Again and Again

When you know the way to track your progress and the different progress you should follow, you now need to figure out how often you will monitor your progress. Tracking your progress just one time every week might be plenty. It might be better to track your progress every two or three days.

By doing this, if you realize that you aren't at where you need to be, you will only have to do a couple days work to catch up. If you just check one time each week, you might get a whole week behind before you realize anything is wrong. What you measure, you can manage. Everyone loves to maintain progress. Each day concentrate on measuring your progress goals instead of your outcome goals. Now, pick a less frequent measurement that you can base on where you are currently at in your project like the distance you have left to your goal or the length you have come from the starting point. With some experiments, you might find a magical balance that will keep you focused.

Stephen Patterson

Chapter 13:
Don't Weigh Pros and Cons

Here is a great way to make hard decisions: find all the evidence about possible outcomes, look at the cons and pros, rationally weigh all these factors, and then make your final decision.

This sounds very straightforward, but anyone that has wrestled with significant decisions that are full of complications found that it isn't that easy. Why? The main reason why is because our brains aren't built to think rationally.

Human psychology is full of shortcuts and biases that help us make decisions quickly. Just like our ancestors had to survive thousands of years ago. When talking about more complex dilemmas now, these cognitive quirks can trip us up.

It is in our nature to get overly obsessed about all the negative things in life. Humans are bad at figuring out cons and pros. Negativity always bothers us more.

Let's look at it this way; you might be the hiring manager at your job. You have been given the task of hiring a new employee. You've interviewed several people and decide to make a list about their negative and positive qualities. Even if you come up with both negative and positives that are equally compelling and relevant, negatives will always carry more weight.

You are going on vacation and are trying to find a hotel to stay at. You have narrowed it down to three possibilities. One hotel has all the amenities you are looking for but has gotten a few negative reviews from people who have stayed there. These negative reviews fill our minds full of doubt. Even if there are more positive reviews, it won't make you rethink your lousy opinion.

Advertisers have used this trick for a long time. They have realized that showing some doubt about competitors could lead customers to doubt their competitor's products and they will no longer buy their products. When making life decisions, this negative bias isn't going to be useful.

How do we fix this cons and pros list? How can we get around this built-in quirk? The first step is to just know that it exists. You can resolve your internal conflicts faster and act quicker by realizing that negative information will always outweigh the positive.

When looking through hotels and you read one comment about how dirty the hotel was, don't let this one comment cause you to doubt your thoughts about how good this hotel will be for your vacation. Remember to look at your cons and pros list again and this time, move your finger onto the side of the positive.

When you can mentally lower how significant the negatives are and bring the pros into the picture more, you will correct your natural negative bias and will be able to make better choices.

Stephen Patterson

Chapter 14:
Keeping Your End in Mind

This just means when you begin something, you need to have a clear picture of what you want and what steps you need to take to get there. If you are always busy, you should do what is important to you.

The basic principle behind it is that things get created twice. The first time is when you create it in your mind. The second is when you do it. Studies that have been done about the Reticular Activating System say that when you can see your goals and are aware of them, your entire energy and talents get activated so you can develop them.

This concept can be used in many areas and contexts in your life such as personal productivity, sports competition, project management, entrepreneurship, and leadership. Coaches will teach athletes to visualize a successful result during an event before they begin the match. If you know how to successfully complete a project, you can plan it out, communicate the idea to other people, and you can measure the success when it gets finished. You are going to have the right motivation to tackle the whole project.

It is imperative that you can visualize a way to plan projects. To access the unconscious and conscious resources that are available to you, you must have a clear picture of what success will look like. There are six steps to help you evaluate your daily progress:

- First one is life. You need to know what your purpose in life is.

- You need to know what your vision is for the next three to five years.

- You need to know what your goals are for the next one to two years.

- You must know what you are responsible for: health, family, job, career, etc.

- What are your current projects?

- What actions are you currently taking?

Things won't happen just because you thought of them. If you just visualize without acting on it, you are only dreaming. Your vision needs to be supported by strategies or plans that will address it adequately.

So, what is your vision in life? The easiest way to get a clear picture is to write down your personal mission statement. Make sure you are clear about whom you want to be, the way you want to live, and the things that give your life meaning.

Conclusion

You now have the tools you need to create healthy habits and stick to your goals to become a successful person. Self-discipline is something so many people are missing, but it is essential to make sure you achieve your dreams. Start creating new habits and get rid of your old bad habits and you're sure to see positive changes in your life.

If you find this book helpful in anyway a review to support my endeavors is much appreciated.

Stephen Patterson

Self-Discipline

www.ingramcontent.com/pod-product-compliance
Lightning Source LLC
Chambersburg PA
CBHW060456080526
44584CB00015B/1445